Celebrating with
FLOWERS

Celebrating with
FLOWERS

JANE ◊ PACKER

PHOTOGRAPHS BY
CHRIS ROBERTS

FAWCETT COLUMBINE · NEW YORK

First published in Great Britain in 1987 by
Pavilion Books Limited
196 Shaftesbury Avenue, London WC2H 8JL
in association with Michael Joseph Limited
27 Wrights Lane, Kensington, London W8 5TZ

A Fawcett Columbine Book
Published by Ballantine Books

Conceived and produced by
Swallow Publishing Limited
Swallow House
11-21 Northdown Street
London N1 9BN

Designer: Jacqueline Palmer
Photographer: Chris Roberts

First American Edition: August 1987

10   9   8   7   6   5   4   3   2

Library of Congress Cataloging-in-Publication Data

Packer, Jane, 1959-
    Celebrating with flowers.

    Reprint. Originally published: London: Pavilion
Books, 1987.
    Includes index.
    1. Flower arrangement.   I. Title.
SB449.P33   1987   745.92   87-47504
ISBN 0-449-90262-5

Printed in Hong Kong

Back flap photograph by Sam Brown.

On previous page, red tulips.

*On page 1, peach roses, primulas, white antirrhinums, blue
hydrangeas and green moluccella (bells of Ireland).*

◊

CONTENTS

◊

To the following people for their continuous help and
support, my parents Maurice and Brenda, my sister Jill,
and especially to Gary, who deserves so much of the
credit yet seldom receives it.

ACKNOWLEDGMENTS

Many people have helped make this book possible, both directly through provided props and venues for photography, and indirectly through giving me the support that provided time to work on it. In this latter respect I am especially grateful to Jayne, Louise, Caroline, Purnima and Lucinda at my shop in London's West End.

For providing venues I am indebted to: Mr and Mrs C. Z. Berger, Jane Foster and Patrick Gottelier of 'Artwork', Joy Goodman, Rosie and Tony Hall, Olivia and Manly Hudson, Joseph Pour la Maison, Joe's Cafe, Mr and Mrs Polemis, Seven Down Street, Andrew Weaving and Ian Thomasson, Phyllis Walters, Joel Wata, Mercia Watkins and Susan Poad for Oscar de la Renta Perfumes, and Whistles. I would also like to thank *Brides* magazine for allowing us to photograph their 1986 fashion show, Andrea Wilkins for a black ballgown, Amanda Curry for her wedding dress, Stephanie Cooper for a dress, Ariane for make-up, and Divertimenti for kitchen equipment.

Various people have helped with the editing and design of the book, and I am most grateful to them for their advice and ideas: Jacqueline Palmer for designing it, Elaine Partington for art direction, Catherine Tilley and Alison Leach for editorial assistance, Tamaris Ryan for checking all the plant names and Adrian Whitely for help in preparing the American edition.

Four books have been helpful in writing the text: *Wedding Customs and Folklore* by Margaret Baker, *And the Bride Wore* by Ann Monsarrat, *Getting Married* by Mary Gostelow and *Bridal Fashions* by Pauline Stevenson.

Sam Brown took the photograph appearing on the back flap and Tim Imrie the photographs appearing on pages 112, 113 and 168. Photographs of the Royal Wedding on pages 86, 120 and 121 were supplied by Mail Newspaper Group PLC, J. S. Library and Camera Press. All other photographs were taken by Chris Roberts, without whose inventiveness and eye the photographs would not have been possible.

INTRODUCTION

THE NATURAL LOOK

A wired posy of dried roses, nigella (love-in-a-mist), hydrangeas and amaranthus (love-lies-bleeding).

Just what is it that inspires a floral designer to forsake a nice warm home in the early hours of a cold wet December morning to go to market, and to do the equivalent of half a day's work while most people are still wrapped up cozily in bed? It's a question I have often pondered as I returned to my shop and faced a day that would not finish before other working people's, despite that early start. But the answer is invariably at hand. Few things can match the thrill of unpacking and preparing the flowers ready for a day's trading, and being overwhelmed by the joy of opening the first box of spring blooms flown in from warmer countries — narcissi, daffodils, tulips, irises, grape hyacinths (muscari) and mimosa — or seeing the rich

beauty of foliage from great English country estates with their deeply colored berries and assorted leaf patterns. But there is more than this; there is the constant pleasure of working with beautiful things and trying to present them as beautifully as possible. A problem arises only when we try to agree on what is beauty in a display.

When I started in floristry, floral design was hidebound and static. It was ready for a change. Too many flower arrangements were statuesque and contrived, looking like poorly conceived sculptural studies. To be fair, this was not only the fault of existing florists. The general public did not demand anything new from us and it was easier to turn out the same old tried and tested designs. The industry was "comfortable," and although standards were definitely improving, this was happening within the confines of established and traditional ideas.

LEFT: *A natural, easy look requires thought and care, as with this seemingly simple arrangement of white arum lilies.*

Since then there has been a revolution in floral design with the growth of the "natural look." The neat and carefully balanced designs of the past are in merciful retreat, giving way to a look that is freer and more dynamic. But what the "natural look" means in practice is not as simple as it may at first seem. It certainly does not mean gathering a handful of flowers from the garden and just plunking them in a jam jar! What it does mean is not so readily defined, and for me it can be understood only in relation to my own history and experience.

At the age of fifteen when asked "what do you want to do?", like most teenagers I didn't have a clue, apart from knowing that it had certainly to be something artistic. The thought of tapping away on a typewriter or spending my days pushing files around from one part of an office to another filled me with horror and didn't fit in with the glamorous future that I was sure was waiting for me just around the corner. School was not a particularly happy experience and therefore the idea of college had little appeal. It didn't really help that my careers officer at school was of the opinion that every girl's ambition should be to be a housewife and mother.

When I was fifteen I started a Saturday job at a florist's close to my home in a small town in Essex, twenty miles from Central London. It paid less than stacking shelves at the local supermarket, but somehow row upon row of canned foods didn't match up to my romantic ideas on my future career. I had always had a trifling interest in flowers, but suddenly, to my surprise, they became absolutely fascinating. The Saturday job that began as a necessity and almost a nuisance turned into the highlight of the week, and on leaving school I started to work full time with a day-release for college. However, at the time the static look in floral design ruled supreme, especially in a small town, so my imagination was hardly going to be allowed to run riot. I can remember being asked to redo the shop window and creating a garden look, replacing the normal stock of dried grasses, vases and plastic pots with terracotta containers, earth and garden tools. After examining it the proprietor deemed that it was too avant garde and told me to dismantle it and put all the normal items back. To be fair, he was right as the locals would probably not have liked it anyway. The prevailing ideas were very old-fashioned. Flowers were definitely regarded as an extravagance, and traditionally people would order them only for births, deaths and marriages. But I started thinking that there must be ways to do things differently.

For one day a week I could escape it all, on my day-release to college in London. The ideas taught there were still traditional, but the girls would talk about their customers spending what sounded like vast sums of money simply for the enjoyment and love of flowers that I had already experienced. So, after eighteen months in suburbia I took myself off to London and found a job in the West End. It was a whole new world. People certainly spent more money and tastes were entirely different.

I continued to work and also study at college for a year before applying for a job as a buyer and florist for a top London hotel. With the offer of the job I was in a position where I could experiment and at last bring my own ideas into the world of traditional floristry. I started to produce displays that were less structured, and with brighter juxtapositions of colors.

When the hotel industry hit a low ebb three years later, budgets were cut all around, and, as is quite usual even now, flowers were particularly vulnerable to these economy measures. My work started to suffer beyond the point which my conscience would accept. Once again I felt frustrated and restless, and began looking around for new opportunities.

I am one of that breed of people whose minds are constantly going off elsewhere. My attention is caught by an object and I am off. I see an antique vase and I start imagining its life story, wondering who has owned it, whether it was a gift, whether it has had sad associations. This quality has served me well in doing flower designs because to keep your ideas fresh, you have to be open to inspiration from unusual sources — perhaps a creeper on the side of a house, an advertisement in a magazine, or the trees in a park. I particularly love vegetables, their shapes, colors and textures. They give me new ways of looking at flowers and sometimes I cannot resist including them in arrangements.

At this time I was luckily exposed to a new source of influence that was very much to affect the way I looked at flowers. As I looked at my other interests, to see if I could happily pursue a career in a different area, I hit upon the varied and complex world of fashion, which is, I suppose, my second love. I was fortunate enough to meet some very interesting and talented people whose energy and enthusiasm seemed boundless. Not all of these people were top-flight designers or established fashion editors. More often than not they were struggling photographers, or make-up artists, carting their portfolios from magazine to magazine, or design students fresh out of college, hoping to sell their collections in order to raise enough money to produce the next. They were often rejected at every turn but would pick themselves up and carry on with the tenacity which brought them there in the first place. It

I get lots of ideas on how to arrange flowers from the shapes plants take when growing in the wild.

Strong color combinations need not look artificial. They exist naturally, as in this view of a magnificent creeper against a blue sky.

was impossible not to admire their dedication and spirit.

Another aspect of the fashion industry that contributes to its innate excitement is the sense of always moving forward or looking forward; there is always something new to discover, always something new just around the corner. It may be a simple variation of or deviation from what has just passed, or something outstandingly different that will capture the attention of the press and through them invite a much wider public to become involved. I knew that this "search" for fresh ideas was what was lacking in floristry.

At this point I began to regret ever leaving the world of flowers. For all the variety and different types of experience that the fashion business could offer me, I realized that there were no other materials to equal flowers. Although texture, color and form are the essence of clothes, a greater diversity is provided by flowers, even the commonly available ones. I began to look for a shop so I could expand my ideas. Ideally I wanted a site in the heart of London's West End where I could not only serve the fashion retailers and designers but hopefully become part of their environment and be seen to be moving along with it.

ABOVE AND RIGHT: *The colors and shapes in fruit and vegetables are a good source of inspiration: combined with flowers, they can be stunning.*

ABOVE: *A truly "natural look"! This urn is piled high with vegetables, fruit, flowers and foliage.*

If my first impulse was to break away from the rigid designs of traditional flower arranging, the lesson of the fashion world was to use that freedom to do the unusual and the novel. There is little point in learning one way of doing things just to get locked into another. Although I loved producing a country-garden look with loose and profuse arrangements, and still do, the "natural look" involves more than always doing this type of design. Its real essence is to use flowers and foliage as their character indicates, so that they do not appear contrived or forced. However, this does not exclude artifice — for example, sometimes wiring a flower can actually make it look more at home than if its stem were left on. Nor does it mean avoiding any props other than a vase and water. Some experts denounce the use of florists' equipment like foam and chicken wire, but these can in fact help us achieve what we want without appearing false. The key thing is the appearance of the flowers — they must look "right."

Hence there are a few principles I try to follow. Foliage should coordinate in both shape and texture with the blooms; do not choose, for example, heavy solid greenery with light and delicate flowers. Containers should be chosen to suit both the flowers and the surroundings that they are to live in. The flowers should be arranged in such a way that they are easy to look at, and do not make anyone strain to find some artistic motivation in the positioning or choice of blooms. The purpose of the flowers is therefore an essential consideration in producing the display. A tumbling arrangement of brightly colored country flowers would look appropriate in an old cottage but would be disastrous in most modern offices or on an intimate dinner table.

One element that receives too little attention is the smell of flowers, possibly because scent has taken third place to color and shape amongst growers. However, the scent of flowers can strike guests long before they can see them strategically placed on a mantelpiece or coffee-table. Here again the occasion is relevant. Wonderful though the scent can be, it will interfere with the smell of food on a dinner table or with the bouquet of wine at a tasting. It can also hang too heavily in a confined space such as a small bedroom.

Although the principles are important, in the end you can only be guided by your eye, and to a lesser extent your nose. What a "natural look" is for me really can be understood only by looking at the flowers, and I hope it is revealed in the photographs in this book. There are many occasions in life when flowers are widely accepted as essential, but many, many more when they will bring a touch of joy to a room and those who use it. The worst you can do in arranging flowers is to interfere with what the flowers will express themselves, and the best is to provide the means to encourage this just that bit further.

This bouquet of grapes, Brussels sprouts, green onions, camellia and ivy foliage, with a single gladiolus, was a brave bride's choice for her wedding.

INTERIORS

To my mind, no room is ever properly "dressed" without some flowers in it, and no other element of interior design offers a comparable prospect of color, texture, perfume and shape in an instantly changeable form. With flowers we can immediately alter the whole feeling of our surroundings, and then change it again the next day if we wish.

In recent years a new concept of how we should live has gained favor. People are more concerned with living healthier and more active lives than before, as is shown particularly in the foods we eat; advertisers have learned the strength of this and constantly use the words "natural and wholesome."

A country look: a basket filled with alliums, scabious and agapanthus (African lilies), flanked by a vase and a basket of amaranthus (love-lies-bleeding), roses and larkspur. In a rural setting one does not only have to stick to flowers — the lilacs and purples in the front basket coordinate with the cabbage leaves.

RIGHT: *A town look: a low-sided basket of blue and white flowers on the coffee-table echoes blue larkspur in two vases on the mantelpiece and picks out the cool blues of the room, thereby emphasizing the orange and pink details.*

This new attitude is not just a matter of conduct, but affects style as well. Models in fashion magazines are not only slim and healthy but wear less make-up than their counterparts of the fifties and sixties. Natural fabrics such as wool, silk, cotton and linen are favored over artificial fibers, despite the practical advantages of these. Casual sportswear is now accepted away from the sports fields and running tracks. Even if we do not exercise regularly, we want to look as if we do!

All this might appear remote from the world of plants, but in fact the flower industry has benefited from this fashion. The accent on health is a response to the need to reduce the stress created by the ever-faster lives we lead, but just slowing down is not held up as the answer. It would seem that we want to look successful, but somehow also to look as if that success has been achieved serenely. Perhaps flowers have been paid more attention by fashion in recent years because they convey both aspects of this image. On the one hand they convey calm and represent the natural world, but on the other they are still considered a bit of a luxury – money is required for exotic out-of-season or profuse displays. Whatever my views on the philosophy of this, as a practicing florist I can only applaud a trend that leads to more and more people making flowers a regular feature of their homes or offices.

When producing flowers for a home or office I aim for a design that appears free, and which harmonizes with the environment. This entails studying the colors of a room and how they fit into an overall design concept. What works for one room will not work in another, however splendid the flowers may be on their own. For example, a huge basket of the most wonderful wild flowers, filled with beautiful foliage, simply would not work in a room furnished with minimal Japanese furniture, not even by virtue of contrast. Such a room, in fact, calls for a few flowers only, or maybe even none at all, but simply a number of twigs or some oriental-looking foliage. Respect for the environment might call for an arrangement that is somewhat contrived in order to complement a deliberately contrived setting. The only proviso is that the flowers are not made to do things that they would not do naturally. This is my golden rule – not to distort the flowers at all, even in the name of making them correspond to their setting.

Apart from that, there are no hard and fast rules for creating stimulating and attractive arrangements. Much that has been written about traditional flower arranging stresses the importance of composition, converging and diverging lines, symmetry and balance. While these critical terms may have a place in the understanding of an artform, they serve no purpose in creation. If you consciously try to follow them, you stifle your instincts and end up with a contrived and regimented display. Moreover, the willingness to experiment gets lost. This is vital, for flowers are highly individual, with no two stems ever being exactly the same. They will never conform with some rigidly predetermined plan of how they must look, so flower arrangers should always be ready to respond to ideas that arise from looking at the cut flowers in front of them. With that flexibility, you need only to take care in choosing the container, look at the décor of the room and think about where the flowers will be positioned.

Despite the need to avoid over-planning I have found that it is no good, when buying flowers for an interior, going to the opposite extreme and just getting whatever appeals on the spur of the moment. You need to have an idea of what you want to achieve, to think of what part of the room you wish to enhance; if the flowers are for a dinner party, it is important to consider also the shape of the dining table and how many people will be sitting around it. Color plays a major part in the choice of flowers, but this need not be the same as the dominant color in the room. You have to look at all its colors with an eye to enhancing certain ones, to see whether there is a particular color that you would like to pick out with the flowers.

Flowers do not have to be overbearing or obtrusive in order to be noticeable. A single beautiful stem in a well-chosen container is often all that is needed to draw attention to, or away from, a feature of the room, particularly with an austere modern décor or modern office. In other settings, such as an eighteenth-century house filled with antique furniture and *objets d'art*, more flowers but equal simplicity can be just as effective – for example, a large urn or fireplace loosely filled with boughs of azalea and rhododendron. As a general rule, the larger the room, the higher the flowers can be placed and the larger they can be. Alternatively, areas of large rooms can be isolated by many small arrangements; a room within a room can be created by grouping color, variety and dimension in one corner, or around an important architectural feature. Similar containers with different flowers in each will provide a note of consistency in an otherwise confused environment.

However much thought goes into the arrangement, it will look careless if any old vase that happens to be at hand is used. Flowers and container should work together to produce a unified appearance. Color compatibility is a fairly obvious consideration but it is also important to think of the shape, including the depth as well as the width of the arrangement, as this

You can always create your
own setting for flowers if the
room seems rather
unpromising. Here a bowl of
peach roses, primulas, white
antirrhinums, blue
hydrangeas, white lilacs in
bud and green moluccella
(bells of Ireland) has been
placed on the bare boards of a
sparsely furnished room and a
piece of matching fabric
draped behind.

has a great bearing on the display. Narrow-necked containers make life simpler as they keep the stems close together with the result that they support each other. On the other hand, vases with very broad necks allow the stems to fall away from one another, leaving a space in the center, and to "roll" at the slightest disturbance. Consequently, wide-necked vases require a proportionately greater number of flowers, or an ample amount of foliage to support the flowers and prevent their falling to the edge.

The container, in fact, provides the opportunity to improvise, for there is no real need to stick to vases or pots designed specifically for the purpose. A hunt around junk shops or second-hand markets will turn up a vast array of inexpensive and unusual china jugs, chamber pots, storage jars and other receptacles. Old perfume bottles and Victorian medicine bottles are a good find for the flower arranger as they make lovely containers for single stems. A bowl with one large bloom either floating in water or just resting on the edge looks beautiful if placed on a low coffee-table or any surface that will be viewed from above. Finally, if a container seems in all other respects perfect for a particular arrangement except that it is too large to give the flowers the support they need, then a wonderfully soft, flowing look can result from putting a jam jar or smaller vase inside it and allowing the flowers to spill over the edge.

Florists' foam (or "Oasis") is useful in deep or awkward containers. Some designers feel that it interferes with the inherent poise of the flower, but it is in fact quite possible to create a natural-looking arrangement with it. Florists' foam supports the stem just as the earth or branch would. It has a further advantage in that being a foam it holds a certain amount of water and presents it to the plant in a similar way to earth. The flower draws as much moisture from the foam as it needs, no more and no less. In contrast, a vase of water is an essentially alien environment to a stem, where it drowns and decomposes. To delay the flowers' demise in it, the stems have to be trimmed about half an inch every two days, and the water must also be changed daily as the rotting stems will deposit particles that alter its chemical nature.

Foliage is a crucial part of an arrangement. Quite apart from its role in supporting flowers, it provides an interesting background and is an important component in its own right, with leaf patterns and shades ranging from dark green to brown to red. Sometimes it is possible to use different types of foliage on their own without flowers at all, especially those that carry berries, such as blackberries, nightshade and elderberries – all quite common and inexpensive (be careful with nightshade as the berries are poisonous). However, if the flower-to-foliage ratio is kept low the flowers must be significant enough to withstand the abundance of greenery. Foliage has one further great advantage for the nervous: if you are worried about cutting too much from the stems of your flowers when trimming them to fit the container, then cutting the foliage first gives you the opportunity to experiment with height and shape.

Some people avoid using long-stemmed flowers in a small vase because they feel that it is somehow "wrong" to cut a flower down. Although it is true that a tall flower may need its long stem to balance the bloom, it is often the case that a flower will be improved by being cut. For instance, amaryllis has the most glorious bloom but a very thick stem that gets coarser towards the base, and no foliage whatsoever. Personally I find it stark and much less attractive when left with the stems at their natural length than when they are trimmed short.

Flowers need not be displayed in just a living or dining room; the kitchen, bathroom or bedroom can be just as effective a setting. We spend as much time in these rooms as any other, and if you like flowers then why not, say, enjoy a small vase of anemones while relaxing in the bath, or a basket of wild flowers when slaving over a hot stove? The heat and humidity of kitchens and bathrooms means that the flowers might not last as long as in another room, and flowers with an overpowering scent are best avoided in a bedroom, but this need not mean excluding flowers from these rooms. A hallway or lobby is an excellent setting, especially when giving parties, as flowers there extend a personal welcome to visitors, giving an immediate indication of your personality and style. And this, ultimately, is what your arrangement of flowers anywhere is meant to suggest.

LEFT: *Brightly colored orange lilies, sunflowers, orange gerberas, and* Euphorbia fulgens *chosen to contrast with the monochrome of the print above.*

LEFT: *Glass case in an orderly office with a black vase filled with lilies of the valley and a phalaenopsis orchid.*

A COTTAGE KITCHEN

Hanging dried flowers and herbs in the kitchen is a sure way of reproducing indoors the feeling of a rambling cottage garden. The smell can be quite strong and is as important as the color.

BELOW: *Blue larkspur, gray poppy seed heads, wild fennel seed heads, sedum, hosta leaves and a mixture of open and miniature roses grouped low in a dark wicker basket create an impression of wildness.*

ABOVE: *Mixed varieties of amaranthus, including the dramatic love-lies-bleeding, their heads positioned as a plant would grow. The terracotta pot adds another contrasting red.*

An uninhibited mass of color from dried and fresh flowers, wild herbs, and vegetation in a country kitchen. Earthenware pots accentuate the rustic feel.

COTTAGE WINDOWS

Nothing enhances flower arrangements more than having sunlight fall through windows onto them. Low bowls or vases on windowsills just catch the rays as they reach into a room. In a small room with limited light, bright colors such as yellow and cream catch and amplify the sunshine.

LEFT: *A display for a summer's day. Glorious warm shades of purple hydrangeas, lilies, larkspur, roses, moluccella (bells of Ireland), tobacco flowers (nicotiana), statice (Limonium latifolium) and Cape marigolds (African daisies) picked out by sunshine in a dark room.*

ABOVE: *Yellow and cream stock and roses, positioned to catch deeper shafts of sunlight penetrating a room, suggest the sunshine itself, as well as here complementing the lace and the beamed walls. In a vase on the windowsill, roses, Kaffir lilies, bouvardia and dahlias echo the patterns of the curtains from inside the room and provide a splash of color against the walls from the outside (left).*

COTTAGE ROOMS

A mass of simple flowers of the same variety or color best harmonizes with the country atmosphere of cottage interiors. Such houses often have low ceilings and small rooms that call for flowers cut short and also placed at a low level so that they are looked down on rather than seen from across the room. Containers should relate to the scale of their surroundings.

LEFT: *Red parrot tulips, salmon roses, miniature floribunda roses, amaryllis, Gladiolus nanus and cream stock reach to a low ceiling.*

RIGHT: *Rose hips, dahlias, anemones and Doris pinks in a large bowl.*

BELOW: *Open anemones cut short for a long bowl echo the colors and texture of mirror frames and a Cologne bottle.*

DRIED FLOWERS

When a lasting display is wanted, dried flowers provide a natural alternative to artificial ones. Their faded and worn image is a thing of the past as modern drying methods — especially freeze-drying and kiln-drying — retain much more color than the old, slower methods. Also, a much wider variety of plants can be dried than used to be the case a few years ago.

Dried and preserved blooms are an obvious choice for the country cottage look. This can be emphasized by using coarsely woven baskets as containers, here placed against a background of pine and faded chintz. Grouping the same flowers together, rather than intermingling varieties, brings out the colors strongly. The flowers shown are the warm reds, purples and creams of amaranthus (love-lies-bleeding), lavender and roses grouped against mustard-colored yarrow (achillea) – colors normally one would hesitate to combine, but capable of producing a bright summery effect.

BELOW: *On its own the basket with the mustard yarrow (achillea) has a gentler, almost elegiac feel.*

C O U N T R Y   L I V I N G

A country garden look can be achieved by gathering
foliage from hedgerows and fields. Not so easily done if
you live in a town, but most florists stock a wide
selection of greenery, and even the average town garden
may yield a surprising range – a rose branch, perhaps,
with rose hips intact; an underestimated privet hedge,
either in flower or the deciduous golden variety;
vegetable leaves; fruit and ivy. The addition of just one
or two modest flowers completes the look.

FAR LEFT: *Pinks, Kaffir lilies and small open roses mixed with green and gold privet.*

LEFT ABOVE: *Pot-marigolds, green sedum, hosta leaves, white roses and yarrow (achillea) massed into a green pot for a rich summer look.*

LEFT. *Tobacco flowers (nicotiana), amaranthus (love-lies-bleeding), moluccella (bells of Ireland), roses, cabbage leaves and ivy set into a genista (broom) basket.*

BRINGING THE COUNTRY TO THE TOWN

Selecting flowers almost at random, as if one had
strolled through a garden picking here and there, can
help to achieve a casual summer look. In reality, it is not
as haphazard a matter as it sounds, and the principle is
to group several varieties and hues together.

LEFT: *Purple larkspur, pink roses, statice* (Limonium latifolium) *and antirrhinums in a blue jug—all chosen to draw out the colors of the furnishings. At one time these plants were available only in summer, but can now be bought throughout the year.*

BELOW: *The tall and willowy larkspur towers above statice* (Limonium latifolium) *that surrounds Cape marigolds (African daisies) resting in and overspilling the rim of the vase. Flowers cut at different lengths resemble garden blooms in a flower border.*

SIMPLICITY IN COLOR

Simplicity, both in the vase and the choice of flowers, can be remarkably effective, even in small displays. If the flowers are not meant to be dominant or are intended for individual enjoyment, or merely if the choice is restricted, then the best display often contains only one variety or one color.

ABOVE: *Drinking mugs in primary colors have been matched with flowers in similar strong hues: purple anemones with bluish-tinged eucalyptus, and red anemones with ornamental peppers and miniature floribunda roses.*

BELOW: *The same idea of using drinking mugs has been adapted for a softer effect. The anemones are mixed and combined with maidenhair fern and blackberries for a look that blends with the muted containers.*

RIGHT ABOVE: *A bowl of open red parrot tulips and eucalyptus has been set on a low coffee-table where the green veining of the petals is intended to complement the colored glass.*

RIGHT: *White tulips placed at the foot of a staircase where the simplicity of their line and color allows the gray veining on the petals to draw attention to the surface of the wood.*

THE DRAWING ROOM

Certain areas in a room used for relaxation can be
emphasized or improved by flowers, and these often
involve wall settings. Often when flowers are placed
against a wall, it is forgotten that they will be seen from
the sides as well as from the front. They need, in fact, to
spread in all three dimensions, not just two.

FAR LEFT: *The splendor of an elaborate gold mirror frame is highlighted with vibrant and clean white lilac, freesias, Euphorbia fulgens,* lilies and eucalyptus, offset by vivid green moluccella (bells of Ireland).

LEFT: *Purple statice (*Limonium latifolium*) and blue cornflowers standing out physically from the wall as well as visually by color contrast.*

LEFT: *Light reflecting in the mirrored table, crystal vase and door handle helps pick out the open amaryllis, lilac, and perfumed tuberoses.*

PERIOD SETTINGS

Flowers should not only complement their surroundings in color or shape but also match any period style a house may have. It can be a challenge to choose ones that look as though they would have been available and popular in a given historical time.

LEFT: *Blue delphiniums, gray eucalyptus, white longiflorum lilies and roses, and blue hydrangeas in a blue glass vase.*

BELOW: *The same table takes on a new warmth with orange lilies set in a bronze glass vase with matching decanter and glasses.*

LEFT: *White carnations and asparagus fern (plumosus), possibly the most despised floral couple of today, can nevertheless be perfect in surroundings where coolness and sophistication are required. In the foreground are hydrangea heads in a bowl.*

RIGHT: *Cymbidium orchids of pink and green, dramatic enough to counterbalance the art deco vases.*

GLASS VASES

Probably the most commonly used type of vase is the tall cylindrical glass one, especially in interiors of a modern style. Although such vases require tall flowers – at least as high again as themselves – the flowers do not have to reach upwards but can be pliable varieties that drape or curve over the rim.

LEFT: *Eucalyptus leaves and buds draped over the edge of a vase.*

RIGHT: *Vivid blue agapanthus (African lilies) with their strong green stems reach from a mantelpiece toward the ceiling.*

BELOW: *Dramatic peach amaryllis teamed with glossy aspidistra leaves stand out against a mutely colored wall.*

DRAMATIC EFFECTS 1

Décor that is strong in line but almost monochrome in color calls for impact. The philosophy behind the choice of flowers is to stay with a clean shape, using one variety, but to let the vibrance of primary colors shine against the surroundings.

Reds immediately draw attention to themselves. Here red tulips are highlighted against a bowl, while the

reflection in a glass table top is particularly striking because the arrangement is not complex and variegated.

RIGHT: *Anthuriums (tail-flowers) pick out the red in the photograph, while the curve of the petals echoes the shape of the chrome table top.*

THE INFLUENCE
OF CONTAINERS

Where the arrangement is to be set against a neutral background, and when the choice of flowers is limited, as it is in early spring, the container becomes very important and is a powerful influence in determining the overall image. Modern vases made of clear glass or in a single strong color call for a minimal variety of color in the flowers, while a basket will dictate a countrified look, with massed flowers cut low.

TOP LEFT: *Irises mixed with similarly colored silvery-blue eucalyptus for a simple but uncompromising vase.*

BOTTOM LEFT: *Three orange parrot tulips with strands of yellow genista (broom) are all that is needed for this tapering black vase.*

LEFT: *Soleil d'or narcissi, lilies, genista (broom) and roses, all bright yellow, with dark green box foliage, in a plain basket suggest the return of spring to the countryside.*

A clear glass vase displays the vivid green of the stems as well as the color of the blooms. The larger vase contains tulips and genista (broom), the smaller one, soleil d'or narcissi.

PURE AND SIMPLE

A single color is ideal for a modest, uncomplicated look where you want the flowers to be pretty but incidental. Such selections should be limited to one or two varieties and placed in a plain container. Harshness can be avoided by using a rounded feminine-looking vase, or by softening the lines of a straight vase by having foliage or soft-stemmed blooms spilling over the rim.

A small mottled blue and white bowl filled with simple white narcissi and marguerites, its roundness echoed by the white arc of flowers.

LEFT: *Ranunculus, tulips and maidenhair fern soften the hard lines of a glass vase as they spill over almost to the glass shelf in a feminine solution to what could be harsh surroundings.*

RIGHT: *Tulips and narcissi add a touch of spring to the hectic life of an office.*

AN EARLY SPRING

When gardens tend to be barren, spring is arriving in
the flower markets of the Northern hemisphere as early
as the end of December. Even though they are still far
off you can remind yourself that warmer days are on
their way with both the fresh colors and the glorious
perfumes of spring flowers.

ABOVE: *Yellow soleil d'or
narcissi, a single lily, a soft
blue iris and nigella (love-in-
a-mist), chosen to repeat the
colors of a pretty decorated
cup and plate.*

ABOVE RIGHT: *Narcissi and
orange ranunculus in a tiny
vase chosen for its band of
matching color.*

RIGHT: *An eggshell blue vase
filled with delicate blue grape
hyacinths (muscari), lilies of
the valley and pink hyacinths.*

ABOVE RIGHT: *Spring's
variety of color is not as great
as that of high summer, but
can be glorious all the same:
tulips, hyacinths, irises and
genista (broom).*

RIGHT: *A dappled china jug
filled with spring pinks,
hyacinths, tulips and
ranunculus. Early buds of
bluey-green nigella (love-in-
a-mist) form a link with the
blue of the vase.*

DRAMATIC EFFECTS 2

Highlighting flowers with spotlights, particularly against angular furniture, reinforces their presence. Again, simple containers and consistency of color and variety are essential to the drama, as to mix colors and types would almost certainly lessen the force of the impact.

LEFT: *Anthuriums (tail-flowers), amaryllis and* Nephrolepis exaltata *fern leaves on a metal table and against a metal screen.*

A silver ice bucket, filled with amaryllis and silvery eucalyptus, teams up well with a tubular-framed side table. A spotlight recreates the shape in silhouette on a bare wall.

THE INFLUENCE
OF THE EAST

Ikebana, the Japanese art of flower arrangement, often aims to express a momentary meaning rather than make a lasting display. Often this is done by using single or small groups of flowers. Ikebana can be both bold and refined, the perfect inspiration when a stark look is wanted. The impulse for this type of display may come from the container, the surroundings, or the assertive character of the flowers themselves.

ABOVE: *With a Japanese décor you have to produce a Japanese-looking display – creating here a display of amaryllis with the stark ridged stems exposed, and individual blooms cut short in a marble bowl.*

RIGHT: *Proteas match the vase and bowl perfectly. To add any other flower would destroy the effect, but a palm leaf and a branch of contorta or corkscrew hazel enhance the oriental feel.*

RIGHT: *An elaborate container like this one calls for simplicity – here two gladioli – rather than a display that would compete with it.*

MATCHING EXOTIC SCHEMES

A décor may be planned thematically around a historical period, a color or, as here, a particular culture. If flowers from the same part of the world are not available, the answer is to interpret the style through color.

The owner of this room collects Africana, so this theme has been picked up with bamboo foliage in the arrangement. Anthuriums (tail-flowers),

"bird of paradise" flowers (Strelitzia reginae) and sunflowers have been chosen as their colors have a strong African feel.

RIGHT: Any flowers put under this Aztec-style mirror need to pick up on the richness and color of gold. This is done by the dominant sunflowers,

which are mixed with papyrus, moluccella (bells of Ireland) and Alexandrian laurel or florist's soft ruscus (Danaë racemosa).

COLOR COORDINATION

Some rooms have such a strong mood and color scheme that the color of the flowers has to follow that of their surroundings. Non-floral elements can introduce that touch of difference that enables the display to stand out nevertheless.

ABOVE: *Silver and gold spray need not be reserved for Christmas! Tree branches sprayed silver and ivy sprayed gold are here grouped with pine, lichen-covered branches, pine cones, apples and grapes in a cool greeny-gray room.*

LEFT: *Preserved purple moss, red fungi and gold-sprayed pine cones against an autumnal fabric.*

RIGHT: *Red anemones, amaryllis and bouvardia selected to emerge from the surrounding reds, browns and golds, when other colors would have shouted out.*

SIDE TABLES

Side tables provide excellent settings in living rooms, though they usually also have other incumbents. It is fine for the flowers to draw a degree of attention to themselves or to their neighbors, but they look crude if they fill the table or obstruct views across the room.

Roses, amaryllis, alstroemeria and laurustinus (Viburnum tinus) *foliage chosen to tone with the room's color scheme.*

LEFT: *Flowers can be larger and taller in a bigger room. Cool whites and greens are never dominant but always look fresh, as here with lilies, amaryllis,* Euphorbia fulgens, *bouvardia and lilac.*

RIGHT: *Cream roses and daffodils low in a silver sugar bowl, bring warmth and distinction to what could easily be a cold and uninviting table.*

LEFT: *Pinks, stargazer lilies and a pink antirrhinum nestling in crystal vases daintily adorn a round table, simultaneously drawing attention to an art deco lamp and blending with the drapes.*

USING ACCOMPANIMENTS

Very often it is not sheer quantity of flowers that makes
the greatest impression, but how they are used and the
accompanying "props." Imaginative containers and
supports are fair adjuncts to the floral designer's art.

FAR LEFT. *Red roses and Euphorbia fulgens with twisted branches of brown catkins. The branches have been extended to entwine the vase and pedestal so as to make a unified arrangement.*

ABOVE LEFT: *A spring display of pink tulips in a container that has been bound with mosses and catkins.*

LEFT: *An antique vase that calls for no more than a minimal arrangement of daffodils, soleil d'or narcissi and blue brodiaea with a few catkins.*

SUMMER DAYS

The warmth of summer can either be welcomed inside
or shut out in a search for coolness, and flowers can
help both of these aims. Where light and heat are
meant to enter the room, a bright range of color can act
as a sort of bridge between interior and exterior, and
when they are excluded, muted tones induce a feeling
of calm.

ABOVE: *Blue and white
heather, thistles, scabious and
agapanthus (African lilies)
match the color scheme of the
room and transmit the
warmth of the garden. The
basket contains yellow pot-
marigolds, white larkspur and
the green tobacco flower
(nicotiana).*

RIGHT: *White stock, mauve
scabious and gypsophila
displayed in a wash jug and
bowl in the coolness of a
bedroom.*

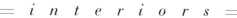

FEATURING THE FORGOTTEN

Carefully selected flowers bring a new character to
blank areas of wall or neglected corners. Where there is
little detail or color the aim is to fill the space with a
display that is interesting in its own right.

*A summer mixture of cream
and white lilies, mauve
scabious, gypsophila, cream
stock and agapanthus
(African lilies) brings life to a
blank area of wall in a living
room.*

*Catkins, longiflorum lilies and
lilac picked to highlight a dark
alcove.*

RIGHT: *A niche in a Victorian
hallway given new status with
gold and cream* Euphorbia
fulgens, *roses and tulips.*

H A L L W A Y S

Hall flowers make the first and the last impression on your guests. Ideally, they should be sufficiently different or imposing to be noticeable without being in any way strident.

Apricot-colored roses, proteas and Euphorbia fulgens, *mixed with grayish-green eucalyptus, have been chosen to complement the carefully color-coordinated tapestry, table and vase.*

RIGHT: *Roses and ranunculus, chosen to make a modest contrast against the amber containers.*

A grand entrance hall deserves something equally impressive. The amber and russets of the gerberas, lilies, peppers, proteas and Euphorbia fulgens *enhance the collection of vases and pots without competing for attention, while this position (below) in front of the mirror gives added depth.*

B A T H R O O M S

Whether *en masse* or a single bloom, flowers are a beautiful if transitory and somewhat unusual accessory to a bathroom. In a pretty, ornate room which suggests leisure they add color and fragrance, while gently introducing a personal touch to clinical interiors.

ABOVE: *A masculine feature is reflected and simultaneously lightened by a simple bowl of pure white tulips.*

RIGHT: *Steel-grays and blues are warmed by massed sweet peas that hang gently over the rim of a rectangular glass vase.*

BATHROOMS 2

One tends to think of bathrooms as having a neutral décor, but often there is one strong feature or color that can provide the starting point for the choice of flowers.

A china shell intended as a soap dish has been placed next to a piece of coral and filled with freesias, amaryllis and narcissi whose whites and creams seem to draw warm tones out of the marble and harmonize with the brass taps.

RIGHT: *Again drawing attention to brass bathroom accessories, a basket of yellow and gold roses, daffodils and poppies, intermingled with white tulips and lilies, repeats and enriches the color scheme.*

PRIVATE THOUGHTS

Flowers in private rooms such as bathrooms and bedrooms seem to introduce a special touch of luxury. Small arrangements are more appropriate, and will give more pleasure, than large impressive ones.

LEFT: *Sweet peas, roses, gerberas, and bouvardia, crammed tightly into a frosted glass vase on a bamboo dressing table.*

Amber and red ranunculus and bouvardia chosen for an unusual touch in a washroom.

LEFT: *A bottle filled with pink bouvardia and set in front of a mirror on a Victorian dressing table.*

BEDROOMS

I normally select bedroom flowers to brighten the room
gently, adding a touch of personality or welcome. Soft
subtle shades, chosen to blend in with what is normally
a quiet décor, are preferable to vibrant colors. Scent
should also be considered: a slight waft can be
wonderful, but a heavy fragrance in a room for sleeping
in is inappropriate.

LEFT: *To add a lot more pink to this child's pale pink room would have risked excess, but a small amount of peach and salmon in amaryllis, roses and poppies increases the warmth of the room.*

LEFT: *A token of spring, with deep blue hyacinths and brodiaea cut low in a shallow bowl.*

BELOW: *Amaryllis, Euphorbia fulgens, longiflorum lilies, lilac and antirrhinums against muslin and lace on a mantelpiece.*

MONOCHROME ELEGANCE

In rooms that are furnished in glass, steel and chrome, color is likely to be minimal, the quality of the materials strong, and line and form predominant. In such surroundings the flowers have to be simple but strong, achieving presence through their height or number. Whites and greens are especially effective, as "natural" colors stand out in austere Modern rooms.

LEFT: *Longiflorum lilies, Euphorbia fulgens, moluccella (bells of Ireland) and papyrus set in a contrasting dark blue vase.*

RIGHT ABOVE: *Longiflorum lilies and Alexandrian laurel or florist's soft ruscus (Danaë racemosa) on the pedestal, complemented by the matching lilies cut short for the table setting in a smart restaurant.*

RIGHT BELOW: *In another part of the same restaurant the lilies have been placed in an ice bucket. The cornflowers on the table are only small but make a dramatic impression in the almost monochrome scheme on account of the vividness of their color.*

FASHION FLOWERS

Restaurants, offices and shops are just as suitable places for floral arrangements as private homes, as in the style-conscious ambience of this fashion business where the color coordination of the flowers is vital.

ABOVE: *Dried giant hogweed, placed in a terracotta urn, in a fashion shop.*

RIGHT: *Gray-green eucalyptus teamed with yellow eremurus (foxtail lilies) to mirror the thick glass inlaid into the floor of the same shop.*

FAR RIGHT: *Red and brown foliage with ornamental peppers and red amaryllis designed to draw attention to the rack of garments.*

TEXTURE

Texture can be as effective as color, if used in the right way. Large rooms decorated in earthy tones may well be spoiled by garish or strong colors, and sometimes fresh flowers are not actually the answer at all.

Large dried heart-shaped fungus, coral, lotus seed pods, fir cones and driftwood selected not only to match the colors of this apartment but also its earthy feel.

RIGHT: *A naturally sculpted tree of gnarled and twisted driftwood stands with sculptures of a more deliberate kind.*

WEDDINGS

Certain wedding flowers have traditional meanings; this bouquet contains roses (love), lilac (first emotions of love), azaleas (temperance), mimosa (sensitivity), and heather. The heather is entwined in trailing ribbons, which were popular features of bouquets in Victorian times.

Even in our supposedly rational and free-thinking age, traditions and superstitions continue to be very much a part of our lives, usually without our being aware of their real meanings and origins. The wedding ceremony is riddled with them, not least in relation to the bridal flowers. Quite often a bride will request certain items to be included in her bouquet or headdress, saying that this is a family tradition – "My mother and her mother both had these flowers in their bouquets." When asked, they do not always know the background to this custom, but it has nevertheless become very important to them. If they but realized, the flowers specified have some particular ancient folk symbolism, and it is quite likely that it is superstition that is at the root of the old family practice.

No doubt, ever since the first bride prepared to take her wedding vows, flowers have been worn in the hair or carried in a small posy as a natural way for a woman to enhance her looks on this most special of days. Flowers also have an association with fertility. There are some references to wedding flowers in classical literature, but the earliest records we have of specific flowers being widely used at wedding ceremonies are from the sixteenth century. The well-to-do Tudor bride would have carried gilded rosemary sprinkled with

RIGHT: *Roses, tulips and amaryllis in a wired bridal posy. They have been grouped closely together to create density of color and texture.*

rosewater, and possibly pot-marigolds and green genista (broom). These flowers almost certainly had symbolic meanings, some of which are known to us. The rosewater added perfume to the rosemary, but may also have been chosen by some because of stories told by travelers and merchants back from Persia. Brides there added it to food and drink in the belief that it would bind their husbands to them faithfully in marriage. Rosemary signified remembrance and would also ward off sorcery. It was especially a fertility symbol, and the nuptial bedchamber would have been decorated with it to guarantee that the marriage was consummated. Fertility would have been symbolized again in garlands of wheat carried by young girls at the wedding, and two boys would have led the procession in the belief that their presence would ensure the birth of sons. Of course, young pages and bridesmaids still feature in weddings today.

Probably orange blossom with its wonderful perfume is the flower that first comes to people's minds in association with weddings. The crowning of both bride and groom with garlands of it no doubt goes back as far as the orange tree itself and is still practiced in Greece; indeed Jacqueline Kennedy and Aristotle Onassis observed the tradition at their wedding in 1968. The orange tree's sweet-scented flowers, dark glossy leaves and fruit are used together, symbolizing abundance and, again, fertility. Other plants used by Greeks and popular today with brides everywhere are ivy, representing the unbreakable bond of marriage, and evergreen foliage, standing for lasting marriage; the wreath or garland itself represents maidenhood or the loss of girlhood.

Orange blossom leads on to another superstition, often disregarded now for reasons of convenience. As orange blossom is not always easy to get, in desperation some people use artificial versions. Putting aside my own feeling about artificial flowers (and florists' windows bedecked with outrageously artificial displays are my pet loathing), there is an old belief that fake flowers must be destroyed within a month of the wedding to prevent good luck from turning into bad. But with the introduction of silk and polyester flowers, more people buy artificial flowers as they can be kept for posterity, and therefore the superstition is tactfully not much observed today.

The list below, which was compiled by a Victorian husband for his wife, includes the meanings of those flowers most often used for weddings. You may want to ponder it if you are about to choose your bouquet; or if already married you may like to know what omens you carried to the altar — especially as not all of them are encouraging!

Acacia, pink	_Elegance_	Lily, white	_Purity and modesty_
Acacia, yellow	_Secret love_	Lily of the valley	_Return of happiness_
Anemone	_Forsaken_	Love-lies-bleeding	_Hopeless, not heartless_
Aster	_Variety_	Magnolia	_Dignity_
Azalea	_Temperance_	Mimosa	_Sensitivity_
Camellia	_Gratitude_	Narcissus	_Egotism_
Carnation, pink	_Woman's love_	Orange blossom	_Purity_
Carnation, red	_"Alas for my poor heart"_	Orchid	_Rare beauty_
Carnation, yellow	_Disdain_	Phlox	_"Our hearts are united"_
Daffodil	_Regard_	Pot-marigold	_Grief, despair_
Fern	_Sincerity_	Rose	_Love_
Foxglove	_Insincerity_	Rose, red	_Bashful shame_
Fuchsia	_Taste_	Rose, white	_"I am worthy of you"_
Honeysuckle	_Bonds of love_	Rose, yellow	_Jealousy_
Hyacinth	_Sport, play_	Rosebud	_Pure and lovely_
Ivy	_Fidelity_	Scabious	_Unfortunate love_
Jasmine, white	_Amiability_	Stephanotis	_"You boast too much"_
Larkspur	_Fickleness_	Stock	_Lasting beauty_
Lavender	_Distrust_	Sweet pea	_Lasting pleasure_
Lilac	_First emotions of love_	Sweet william	_Gallantry_
Lilac, white	_Youthful_	Tuberose	_Dangerous pleasure_
Lily	_Majesty_	Wood hyacinth	_Constancy_

Probably the Victorians were the greatest enthusiasts for giving meanings to flowers. They earnestly adopted folk beliefs and added some of their own, usually romantic ones, so that nearly all common flowers came to stand for something. They then used the flowers to convey messages to the objects of their love. Similarly, wedding bouquets may well have been made up in special combinations according to these meanings, and I think these may lie behind most of the family traditions that I hear about from brides-to-be.

This bride's loose tresses have been caught up with a romantic circlet of pastel-colored blooms. The young bridesmaid dressed in peach carries a large tied bouquet of orange lilies.

A bouquet of creamy-pink tulips tied with a large bow and held loosely in the arm. They are matched with just a couple of blooms pinned into the hair.

BRIDAL FLOWERS

I have always especially enjoyed preparing flowers for weddings, from my first days in floristry. The possibilities are particularly exciting, for fashion and tradition jostle for predominance in the design. At the same time there is plenty of room for individual taste and preference, as well as the chance to encourage clients to adopt ideas that might not have occurred to them.

Floral decoration for weddings falls into four broad categories: bridal flowers (including the bridesmaids), flowers for the ceremony, flowers for the reception, and flowers for the groom and guests. The flowers for the bride and bridal party are usually given the highest priority, and as the bride will be the focal point for most of the day, it is right that the bouquet and headdress should be considered first. They therefore provide the basis from which to identify a general theme or style that can run through all the flowers.

The purpose of identifying such a theme or style is not to stick dogmatically to it, but to use it as a springboard to improvise and develop ideas. The starting point is often the color or design of the dress chosen by the bride, but it may equally well be something much less precise. There might be a distinct theme to the wedding, such as Victoriana, with the bride and groom wearing Victorian dress. At the first meeting the florist should establish the theme, and at the same time take note of the height of the bride, her complexion, hair coloring, and personality. Some brides have quite definite ideas of what they want and the florist can only make suggestions on how to modify or build on them. But often at this early stage the bride's plans are not highly formed, and ideas develop and grow from the initial conversation.

The style of wedding planned will usually be determined by the personality of the bride, and this in turn will give the clue as to the flowers that are needed. If the bride is romantic and opting for a floating and full dress made of fine silk that rustles and sways with the slightest movement of the layers of petticoat, then puffs of misty gypsophila and pastel pinks, lilacs, whites and creams are likely choices. But a young, highly fashion-conscious woman who is not going for a traditional wedding, even if she is contemplating a religious ceremony, is likely to be looking for something individual, especially if she has chosen a dress that is not specifically designed for a wedding. A traditional bouquet is then out of the question, and I might start thinking of one composed of unlikely shades grouped together in a vibrant combination — pinks, oranges, purples, reds and yellows — or possibly just strong reds.

A flowing bouquet is also unlikely to be suitable for an elegant person who disdains ribbon and lace and relies on couture line and detail. Simplicity would be my first thought, and we could end up with two stems of longiflorum lilies bound with a generous bow, and a large headdress of bold individual lilies in a garland worn low on the forehead. On the other hand, someone who prefers a quiet ceremony with a limited number of guests may wish to carry only a small posy.

Once the overall style is established, the next stage is to look in detail at the wedding dress, bridesmaids' dresses, and trimmings. Color is vital, but people have varying perceptions of shades and hues — one woman's ivory is another woman's cream — so it is not good enough to rely on a verbal description. If they have not already been supplied at the first meeting, I ask for a sample of the fabrics of the dresses and of the ribbons or lace used for trimmings. With these I can set about choosing flowers that will tone with the dress.

When the overall style of the wedding and the details of the dress fabric and trimmings have been determined, and some knowledge of the bride's personality has been gained, the florist can then get on with designing the bouquet and the headdress (if there is one). With the bouquet, apart from the question of color, there is the shape to consider, and how rigid it should be. Of course, wedding bouquets have changed enormously over recent years, due not only to the influence of fashion but also to the introduction of various modern materials and the much wider range of flowers found in the market today thanks to air transport. Until about thirty years ago the average bridal bouquet would have contained roses, carnations or lilies, with the stems left intact and wired into moss, often in a huge shape almost overshadowing the bride. Since then they have become much smaller due to the improvements in florists' materials and techniques.

Whatever its size, I always try to make a bouquet look uncontrived even though individual leaves and petals may be supported by very fine wires. The stems are removed mainly because they are less flexible and heavier than wires. A normal stem cannot be bent or twisted like a wire, and a wire can be chosen to a gauge just strong enough to support the flower. A bridal bouquet should be light, as a heavy one will hamper the bride, look uncomfortable and may ruin the line of the dress. (Similarly, a heavy corsage will drag down on a delicate fabric.) However, the wiring should not be obvious, and the flowers should still retain their natural movement. To achieve this skill requires many years of practice and should always be left to the professional.

A favorite alternative of mine is "looser" bouquets that are not wired at all. In recent years I have begun to make a feature of tied bunches of flowers with the stems still intact. This attracted quite a lot of publicity as an alternative to the traditional bouquet, and many a bride-to-be came into the shop drawn by the idea but not quite convinced that an unwired bouquet was right. However, more people now accept them as they provide adaptable and natural-looking arrangements.

A loosely tied bouquet of white tulips and gypsophila. The half-circlet headdress contains white lilac.

Another welcome shift in taste in recent years is towards headdresses of fresh flowers. Artificial flowers never look right, and seen in conjunction with real flowers in the bouquet can easily spoil the whole appearance of the bride. Many women decide against fresh flowers because they fear that they will not remain in good condition throughout the day. This is a reasonable anxiety, and one could either go for a headdress of dried flowers or make one from the dress fabric. However, there are flowers that will last the course well and a florist may recommend, for example, orchids, freesias and stephanotis. Also, the way they are wired can help to keep them erect. I would not pretend that the flowers will look as fresh at the end of the day as they did when they were put on, but they will have been the perfect match to the bouquet, and they will certainly have looked much lovelier than any of the alternatives.

When making a headdress, much the same principles apply as to the bouquet, in terms of matching the style and colors of the dress and the bride's personality. There is also the added consideration of the hair; there is no point in deciding on a certain type of headdress despite the fact that the hair is too long, too short, too thick or too fine to support it in place, and to find that the bride spends all day worrying about it slipping. The safest options are the circlet and the headband.

The advantage of the circlet is that the back of the bride's head is going to be viewed by the guests for most of the ceremony, so flowers here will be well featured. The flowers can be placed without using a full circlet by weaving a horseshoe shape that thins out towards the tips and just touches the cheekbones, or by attaching flowers to a comb just above the veil.

A headband is a good choice for young bridesmaids, as little girls usually have fine hair which will not provide much hold for pins and hair-grips.

Whatever flowers have been chosen for the bride, the colors and varieties should be carried through to the bridesmaids' flowers unless they are wearing a different color from the bride. Little girls look delightful carrying novelty arrangements such as pomanders, but for grown-up bridesmaids it is better to opt for a smaller version of the bride's bouquet.

An example of all these considerations in operation is the wedding of Sarah Ferguson to Prince Andrew in July 1986. Although it was a great thrill and responsibility to be asked to do the bride's flowers, in many ways it had to be handled like any other commission.

We met several times to discuss the flowers, and it soon became clear to me that Miss Ferguson is an independent and inventive person, with a lively character and good sense of fun. Although tradition was going to be respected, she wanted the flowers to reflect her individuality as much as possible. For instance, she did not want the bridesmaids' flowers to be at all run-of-the-mill. I saw the outfits that they were to wear and at first we discussed using pomanders as they would fit with the dresses and the pages' sailors' outfits perfectly. Then the picture of Victorian children playing with hoops popped into my mind, and seemed the ideal things to use. A side benefit was that they turned out to be very easy for the children to carry. Because of their firm base they could be swung around and carried quite naturally to the Abbey and down the aisle.

With the headdress and bouquet we had to match the overall color scheme of peach and cream. This is not as easy as it sounds since there is not a wide range of commercially grown flowers that are definitely either of these colours, and two supposedly cream blooms can look totally different when put together. Another factor was that I was asked not to use any foliage in the bouquet, although this is a sound way of creating texture and depth. Instead I had to produce these qualities by using a variety of flowers of different shapes and sizes. There was a further stipulation that all the flowers should be perfumed. This proved to be limiting because many commercially grown flowers do not have a scent as growers have instead developed longevity, size and color. The final selection could not be made without a piece of the wedding gown, so as to get the right shades of cream. Eventually I decided on lilies of the valley, cream lilies, cream roses and gardenias, all shaped into a long trailing bouquet.

Miss Ferguson wanted to wear her veil after the wedding ceremony, which considerably influenced the design of the headdress. We felt that rather than fuss around removing the flowers and veil, and then putting on the tiara, which would inevitably involve re-doing her hair, it would be much easier if the tiara were worn throughout the ceremony with a headdress large enough to cover it. The veil was then to be stitched to the headdress so that it could all be lifted off in one piece to reveal the tiara beneath. As it happened, this fitted in with my original idea which was for the headdress to be a half-circlet of large blooms worn low on the forehead. It seemed to be appropriate for the bride to get away from the dainty pretty look and opt for a more bold, almost Pre-Raphaelite beauty.

The Duke and Duchess of York in the Abbey: I emphasized line and lightness in the bouquet so as not to conflict with the heavily beaded gown. The various shades of cream provide the density that might otherwise have been created by foliage.

Summer flowers — peonies, larkspur, stock and Alchemilla mollis
(lady's mantle) — in a traditional church pedestal arrangement.

FLOWERS FOR THE CEREMONY

The decoration of the church, synagogue, or other place where the wedding is to be held, is often an afterthought, the flowers there not being considered as essential as the bridal bouquet. Nevertheless, flowers can make a huge difference to such a building, and can be chosen to augment those the bride is carrying. Although you cannot get away from the fact that the more there is to spend, the more spectacular the flowers are going to be, a limited budget should not be the reason for excluding the scene of the ceremony totally.

In such cases the florist can produce a striking effect with a single large arrangement that will be noticed straight away; you do not have to parcel out the financial allocation into several small displays that will be lost in the spaciousness — and possibly darkness — of a church or synagogue.

When the florist is given sufficient scope, one consideration is the very special atmosphere that people generally feel when entering the precincts of a religious building. It can be effective to proclaim the coming wedding at the gates by tying on bows entwined with ivy or other flowing foliage. Picking up the theme, garlands placed on the doors in the style and color of the flowers inside hint at what is to come, and introduce a note of festivity and welcome to a building which may be unfamiliar to many of the guests, and possibly somewhat austere.

Certain areas in the church or synagogue are obvious sites for floral arrangements: the altar, the pulpit or chuppa. But these are not the only parts of the building where flowers can be placed — pew ends and pillars easily lend themselves to wonderful and unusual effects. However, flowers should complement, not dominate a building, therefore it is a good idea to place the main arrangements to one side so as not to compete with existing features. They should become part of the building and look as if they belong to it, but should not be so subtle that they become insignificant.

· White flowers are probably the most popular choice for decorating buildings for weddings. English churches in particular, beautiful as they are with shafts of light falling from high stained glass windows in small pools, tend overall to be dark, with those pools of light being colored by the windows. White flowers in such places introduce a light and airy feel. However during the winter months white can intensify a feeling of coldness, and then reds, apricots, and pinks mixed together are a better choice so as to suggest a warm summer's day, or yellows, creams and bright greens for a hint of spring.

Blues are always difficult to interpret and if possible should be avoided when decorating dimly lit buildings, as they tend to fade and disappear. If, however, a bride insists on blue as an integral part of her color scheme to tone with, for example, the bridesmaids' dresses, then the lighter the shade, the better. Pinks, cerise, or purples surrounding it help to promote the color.

Again, the choice of the actual variety of flowers and colors must reflect the style of the wedding. The girl who is marrying in a broderie anglaise or muslin dress would almost certainly want a relaxed uncomplicated feel to the day. Simple flowers such as daisies, anemones and sweet williams are more appropriate to this approach than the more stylized hot-house or imported blooms such as stephanotis or orchids. For a country feel, I would go for uncomplicated flowers and mix them with nature's own indiscrimination — yellow, pink, orange and purple.

Many religious buildings no longer encourage paper confetti because of the mess it creates, particularly if there are two or three weddings in a day. An inexpensive and, I think, far nicer alternative, is either to cut flowers from the garden that are past their best or visit a flower stall that sells cheaper flowers of less high quality. Strip the petals off and shower the bridal couple with them. It is still a good idea to consult the minister or groundsman, but they rarely object to a pathway of beautiful petals that will return naturally and much more quickly to the earth than paper confetti does.

A mixture of lilies, moluccella (bells of Ireland), roses, Euphorbia fulgens *and chrysanthemums set in a pedestal arrangement.*

*Selections of flowers and foliage placed low in vases for table
settings in a magnificent garden.*

THE RECEPTION

Except for intimate receptions with just a few guests, where the only flower decoration would be of the kind one might provide for an ordinary home display (see previous chapter), there are various principles that apply to providing the flowers for any size of formal reception, whether at home or in a hired room or hall.

Firstly, the position of the flowers is as important as their size, and inextricably related to it. Particular care has to be taken with hotel function rooms and halls, which can be conversely impersonal or so highly decorated as to leave little room for individual expression. As a general rule the flowers should be placed so as to draw the eye either towards or away from a particular aspect of the room. This might mean decorating the mantelpiece or draping garlands from a central pillar so as to avoid a strong decorative scheme below. Moreover, reception flowers often have to be high up, especially if the guests will be standing for drinks and canapés, as it is pointless filling the hearth

of a fireplace with a wonderful arrangement if the people can only see across the room at shoulder level.

The gently billowing canvas of a marquee provides a marvelous setting for high arrangements, for the central poles always look wonderful with flowers cascading from them. Equally effective are hanging baskets on long chains either suspended from the roof or around the edge where the awning hangs, filled with cut flowers or summer flowering plants such as lobelia, trailing geranium and nasturtium.

Secondly, tables, whether they are being used for formal eating or for serving buffets, cry out for flowers. Food and flowers enjoy a particularly special visual relationship, and a word with the caterer will usually inspire a good deal of enthusiasm. Flowers do not only have to be placed in containers; fresh petals can be scattered across a buffet table, with the colors mixed, or shiny-surfaced leaves can be pinned to the table-cloth with clusters of grapes, apples and oranges.

Seating arrangements will greatly influence table decoration. Space can be a problem if the guests are to sit either side of long, narrow tables adjoining the bridal party at a head table. Once the cutlery and other tableware are in place, there is only a very narrow area along the center in which to put flowers. One solution is to lay a very thin garland made of various foliages and entwined dainty blooms in the space and to let it spill over both sides when it reaches the head table. It can then be continued along the front of the head table and draped over the cloth, caught up with clusters of flowers or large white bows. If candles are to be used, candelabra can be surrounded by flowers. This will raise the decoration above eye level so as not to interfere with the guests' vision as they chat to one another.

If only the head table or buffet is to be decorated, then a real feature must be made of it. Again, I often use garlands of flowers and foliage or trail smilax *(Asparagus medeoloides)* looped along the table's length and caught up with clusters of fruit and blooms. Miniature flowering trees at the ends of the table, or tall plants with thick foliage, lend perspective to the scene.

The color scheme or theme of the wedding should of course be carried through to the reception: you don't have to give up if the budget for floral decoration is minimal, but harmonization with the other elements becomes important. If, for example, the bridesmaids' dresses and bouquets are pink, a few single-stems or small vases on pink table-cloths are sufficient – or the same flowers with pink napkins and candles on a white table-cloth.

Lastly, the cake, as a major feature of the wedding feast, must certainly be decorated with flowers of some kind. Many wedding albums include pictures of the happy couple cutting the cake with the bride's bouquet lying in front of it, alas showing that the opportunity to crown it with similar flowers has been missed. If there are several tiers to the cake, I add small clusters of flowers between or around the dividing pillars, and also to the base of the cake so as to balance the color at the top. The cake table itself can be decorated in the same way as the buffet table, with garlands and foliage or perhaps with a 'cloth' of shiny leaves such as ivy, galax (wandflower) or cherry laurel.

High up in a marquee the poles have been decorated with green and white flowers, and between them hangs a basket with the same flowers cascading from it.

FLOWERS FOR THE GROOM, BEST MAN AND GUESTS

It is not as common now as it once was to give each guest a buttonhole to wear for the day; indeed, in some countries this has never been the custom and flowers are not normally worn by guests at all. Most bridal couples do, however, present the immediate family, best man, and ushers with a buttonhole of some description, and the groom will have chosen something for himself. Once again, the chosen color scheme can be repeated; for instance, if the bride is carrying peach roses then why not choose a peach rose for the groom

and best man? However, to give peach-colored flowers to the ushers and other male guests might be overdoing it, so it would be advisable to give them white or cream roses, or roses of a different shade of peach. This would distinguish the groom and best man from the remainder of the party. The use of asparagus fern (plumosus) as a backing has become a cliché, but other foliages can be used, or even leaves from the rose itself or the ivy used in the bride's bouquet. The latter will look stronger and more masculine.

The mothers of the bride and groom are usually given a corsage to wear: a small shaped cluster of wired flowers, light and dainty enough for it to be easily pinned to a delicate fabric, and either matched or contrasted to their outfits and accessories. If one does not know in advance what the outfits will be, then it is safest to choose neutral colors of, say, white or cream, that hopefully were chosen for the bride's bouquet. The bride's mother's corsage is often the only item, aside from the bride's bouquet, that is made to a very personal combination. There is, however, another tradition that I think is also a nice gesture which is to include most of the kind of flowers used in the bouquet.

Once considered an old-fashioned and traditional gift to mothers and close relations at a wedding, corsages have been revamped and are no longer unfashionable. This is a corsage of roses, Singapore orchids and genista (broom).

For a florist weddings are a constant source of inspiration and challenge. Sometimes I feel somewhat stifled by the essentially traditional nature of the event and the limitations imposed, but maybe this is a good thing – after all it is not *my* wedding. Nevertheless, for all the tradition behind the ceremony, my message to future brides is that if you want the best from your flowers and your florist, be bold and courageous. This does not mean that you will end up with something outrageously avant-garde, but something that most agrees with who you are and what you really want for the day.

BOUQUETS 1

Small and dainty bouquets would be lost in the opulence of large, floating wedding dresses, and wired bouquets might appear rigid and unsympathetic to the movements of the dress. The solution is often to go for a loosely structured tied bouquet of large blooms with unwired stems.

Purple and blue delphiniums mixed with gray eucalyptus in both the headdress and the loosely tied bouquet.

Stargazer lilies, tulips and asparagus fern (sprengeri) move gently with the swish of a full skirt. Sophisticated flowers were selected to go with the richness of the dress fabric. The headdress consists of just stargazer lilies.

LEFT: *Coneflowers* (Rudbeckia nitida) *and lilies were chosen for their strong gold color so as to draw attention to the yellow detail on the waist and a large yellow bow at the back of the dress.*

B O U Q U E T S 2

Although soft pastels will probably always be the favorite choice of brides, splashes of strong color, standing out against the bridal gown, are more appropriate for an assertive look and can be quite startling. If the bride feels happy with this effect, it can go well with romantically styled dresses.

RIGHT: *An eye-catching sheaf of red Singapore orchids and red roses, to be carried low or over the arm. The looseness of the unwired bouquet matches the full flowing style of the dress, while the red stands out dramatically against the white material.*

CENTER: *A tightly massed bunch of red anemones, amaryllis and mixed foliage. It was made to be held at waist height. The bouquet does not interfere with the close-fitting line of the gown, but rather has been designed to accentuate it.*

FAR RIGHT: *Unusual choices of bridal flowers can nevertheless be successful, especially if a striking look is wanted as with these bold red anthuriums (tail-flowers) carried with an untraditional dress.*

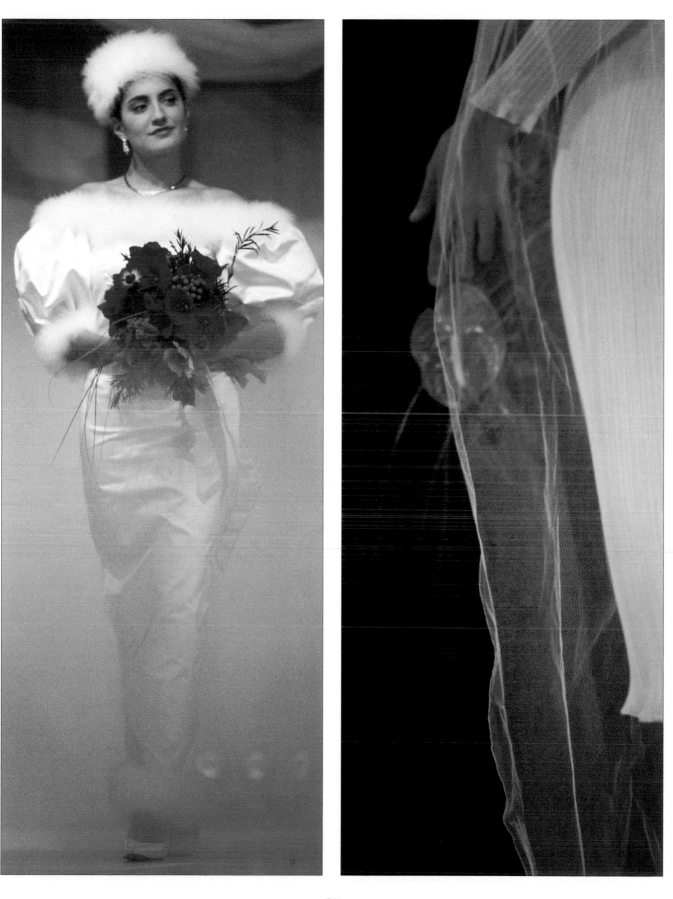

B O U Q U E T S   3

White remains by far the most popular color for a bridal gown, and will probably always be so. While bright flowers stand out vividly against it, soft colors, and white itself, further the air of romance. They often gain prominence through contrast with the overall shape and the detailing of the dress.

Pastels for bride and bridesmaid – cream and pink roses, scabious and asparagus fern (sprengeri) tied into the shape of a posy for the bride.

RIGHT: *The traditional veil and train here take on a new appearance, calling for a posy (of cream roses and hydrangeas) that balances the vastness of the headdress.*

LEFT: *White roses and amaryllis, chosen so as not to compete with the fabric detail and embroidery of the dress.*

ABOVE: *Stark and dramatic, a single open white lily and palm leaf, tied with a white satin bow is the perfect complement for an elaborate dress.*

VARIATIONS ON TRADITION

From time to time a florist will be dealing with a bride who does not want to dispense with the traditional dress, bouquet and headdress altogether but wants a radical variation on them. This change may be in the design or color of the gown, the content or shape of the bouquet or the form of the headdress. Whatever it is, it will call for some original thought in the flowers.

ABOVE: *Roses, ranunculus, azaleas, lilies, ivy and rose hips in an unusually large headdress. This arrangement both complements the unconventional dress in color, and provides an extravagance to counterbalance its plainness. The whole color scheme has an early autumnal feel.*

ABOVE AND RIGHT: *One could not be further away from the traditional color of a bridal gown. Only red flowers could work with the drama of the black outfit; moreover, there have to be plenty of them. Red amaryllis, anemones and amaranthus (love-lies-bleeding) frame the bride's face and tumble from her arms.*

A range of colors and shapes of tied and wired bouquets, posies, circlet and horseshoe, suitable for bride and bridesmaids. The individual arrangements are described on the following pages.

Open and miniature cream roses, gold and russet shades of ranunculus, creams and greens interspersed with ivy leaves and trails, and sprigs of hebe in a wired posy for a late summer wedding.

Anemones, tightly bunched and tied into a posy, together with a circlet of the same, free of any foliage other than their own so as not to impinge on the colors of the blooms.

Different shades of pink in roses, Doris pinks and ranunculus together with wispy strands of gray santolina foliage to draw attention to the green tints of the ranunculus buds and the green veining of the tulips.

RIGHT: *Peach-colored amaryllis, poppies and primulas wired into a posy with green primula leaves* *emphasized by green ribbon trails. A horseshoe gift of white heather also with peach-colored primula flowers.*

LEFT: *Traditional bridal bouquet shape, known as a shower bouquet, made up of longiflorum lilies, miniature cyclamen blooms and leaves, Alexandrian laurel or florist's soft ruscus* (Danaë racemosa) *and silver-leaved* Senecio maritima *foliage.*

A good choice for bridesmaids of all ages and a good match for a bouquet like the one opposite, as it contains a more modest selection of rosebuds and marguerites.

CHURCH FLOWERS 1

Unusual parts of the building easily can be featured
without having to use large amounts of flowers. Often
more is said by the choice of material than the quantity.

*A large bow entwined with
gypsophila and ivy on the
gateway of a church
announces a wedding.*

RIGHT: *Strands of hops climb
around a pillar in a city church,
introducing a sense of living
nature into an old building.*

CHURCH AND SYNAGOGUE

Flowers should either emphasize or embellish
architectural features, but not work against them,
unless the setting is such that it recedes from an exces-
sive display.

LEFT: *A major focus point in a Jewish wedding, this chuppa has been grandly decorated at the four corners of the canopy to bring a profusion to a modern building. The white flowers – agapanthus (African lilies), delphiniums, gerberas, gypsophila, larkspur, longiflorum lilies and roses – imply purity.*

Pedestal arrangements of singing colors of delphiniums, dahlias, gerberas and stock lead the eye to the splendor of a stained-glass window.

CHURCH FLOWERS 2

The problem with large buildings is choosing what to
decorate. I usually set out to concentrate on the areas
most noticed during the ceremony or on arrival, and
make a splash around each.

LEFT: *A complete color
spectrum of summer flowers
brings a country feel to a city
church – pink antirrhinums,
Alchemilla mollis (lady's
mantle), bulrushes,
carnations, echinops (globe
thistle), white larkspur,
peonies and pink statice
(Limonium suworowii).
Copper-beech foliage supplies
depth.*

LEFT: *The aisle and altar of
the church.*

RIGHT: *In the same church,
mauve cornflowers,
gypsophila, peonies, pinks
and pink statice (Limonium
suworowii) flow from the top
of the pew end to the floor.*

THE RECEPTION. 1

For a grand reception in ornate surroundings the
flowers need to be muted but warm, not risking
overbearance by competition, but sufficiently abundant or perfumed to make an impression.

LEFT: *Agapanthus (African lilies), bouvardia, delphiniums, fennel, gerberas, larkspur, lilies, roses and perfumed tuberoses massed with foliage.*

RIGHT: *For the reception, the same flowers are used in a different arrangement, placed high on ornate gold stands to lead guests to the reception area.*

RIGHT: *Consistency in the choice of flowers when there is a large space to decorate brings a unity to the occasion, like a theme running through a piece of music. Variety comes from the sitings and arrangements. The flowers here trail towards the hearth from a mantelpiece.*

THE RECEPTION 2

The choice for the table decorations should continue the color scheme established by the larger display. In the more intimate setting of the meal, the motif that has already been established in the rooms where the guests have been received should be repeated. Centerpieces should either be low or in candelabras so as not to interfere with people's lines of vision. For evening receptions the flowers may well be accompanied by candles.

LEFT: *Solid, shiny cherry laurel leaves with roses, lilies and spray carnations around two large candles in an opulent dining room.*

BELOW: *Roses, miniature carnations and scabious held aloft on candelabra and echoing the displays on the mantelpiece.*

THE RECEPTION 3

This wedding was held in the height of summer and greens and whites were selected for the marquee in order to provide a cool look in the shade. The tables on the lawn have jugs of flowers picked from the garden.

ABOVE: *A lovely outdoor setting needs little embellishment. Here some garden flowers on the tables are all that is necessary.*

RIGHT: *Gypsophila, longiflorum lilies, larkspur, roses and an abundance of foliage around one of the poles of the marquee.*

A ROYAL WEDDING

With millions of people around the world watching, it was essential that the headdress and bouquet for the wedding of Sarah Ferguson and Prince Andrew on 23 July 1986 would remain bright and fresh. The flowers had to match the peach and cream color scheme, which created difficulties as different "cream" blooms can be quite unalike in color when put together. Although I designed the bouquet it was actually made, as is traditional for royal weddings, by the Worshipful Company of Gardeners.

RIGHT: *Young bridesmaids' flowers have to be resilient as they are not always handled with the greatest care! The hoops gave the flowers a firm base and were easy for the children to carry. However, the basic frames had to be specially made, and after several attempts were only ready at the eleventh hour. They were then bound tightly with peach ribbon. Both hoop and headdress consist of floribunda roses, carnations, lilies of the valley and freesias.*

ABOVE: *The first glimpse of Miss Ferguson as she leaves for the Abbey. Both headdress and bouquet consist of lilies, gardenias, roses and lilies of the valley. There is no foliage in either by request, and only fragrant flowers were used.*

RIGHT: *Re-appearing with her husband, the new Duchess of York has removed the floral headdress to reveal the diamond tiara that signified her change of title.*

SPECIAL OCCASIONS

Normally, as I have stressed before, flowers should complement a room rather than dominate it. But parties and festivals like Christmas or Thanksgiving are exceptions as the flowers can be used to superimpose the event on the existing décor.

There are two factors that should determine party flowers. Firstly, if there is a theme to the party it should be employed fully, even exaggerated so the guests can't miss the point. One must remember that when a room is filled with people any decorations are considerably less noticeable. Even if there is no obvious theme to the occasion, a style or mood could be chosen which the decorations can reflect. Secondly, one should use the positive points of a venue to full advantage and not try to crush its personality. A strong style or atmosphere in a room should be a guide and the flowers should not actually conflict with the décor despite the need for them to establish a strong presence.

There are obvious ideas for decoration, such as using predominantly red flowers throughout a Valentine's Day celebration. Alternatively, you might develop a more general theme to run through an occasion. For example, a winter party could be decorated with tree branches carrying rich fungi and lichen growth, or twigs sprayed white and draped with ivy to make an interesting background. For a suggestion of spring, mantelpieces could be given banks of moss, and daffodils, hyacinths, tulips and grape hyacinths (muscari) grouped as if emerging from winter soil. Dining or buffet tables can echo the mood with thickly woven baskets holding the same varieties of flowers and filled with bun moss.

Red roses, Euphorbia fulgens, *ornamental peppers and berries against a Victorian screen. Red and green are so commonly associated with Christmas that it is difficult to get away from them for the festival, but it is nevertheless possible to introduce out-of-the-ordinary elements that make a display distinctive.*

Longiflorum lilies, white Euphorbia fulgens, *lilac and tulips mixed with foliage, designed for a winter cocktail party.*

Sometimes, however, the style of the room will have to govern the choice of even party decorations. I was once asked by a leading fashion magazine to decorate the venue of their party. "Vases of white flowers only" were requested, but when I saw the building I knew immediately that a classic and tasteful floral design would be totally wrong. The venue was a fashionable night-club with chintz wallpaper, wrought-iron scroll-work and flock just about everywhere else – a style representative of decadent European nightlife in the thirties and forties. So we decided to work with the club's existing design, not against it. We covered wrought-iron stands with fruit sprayed gold to imitate the cornices around the room, and gold vases were used with twists of red and gold brocade fabric entwined about them and their stands. In these vases we arranged the flowers most popular in the thirties – deep red roses and carnations intermingled with asparagus fern (plumosus). Though not considered fashionable now they were just right for this *kitsch* occasion.

For an informal party where there is no guiding theme or dominant style of venue, there is the freedom to do what you will. A bland empty room could be turned into a garden by placing young trees in pots in the corners, massing trails of ivy, jasmine and honeysuckle above doors and from ceilings, even introducing a fake pond surrounded by banks of moss, pebbles and plants. Tables can be covered with simple cotton or gingham cloths and any other accessories which could complement the flowers and foliage included.

When it is a formal occasion, the flowers should be more restrained and arrangements restricted to certain areas. An immediate impact can be made with a large arrangement placed where guests will be greeted. It is important to use areas where vision is likely to be directed: dining tables are an obvious focal point, and low-hanging overhead lights or wall lights, mirrors and large pictures are also good sites. If the guests will be standing for much of the time it is a good idea to position the flowers on any suitable room features at eye level.

One big dining table can be decorated with large candles mingled with arrangements of flowers of various heights and standing on a silver tray to reflect the candlelight. Another idea would be to place a small individual arrangement next to each guest's wine glass, or entwine small twigs with a few flowers or sprigs of foliage as a base for a place setting card.

CHRISTMAS

Of all the seasonal festivals, Christmas is the one when people most think of introducing flowers into the home. With the fresh pine trees and evergreens that make up traditional Christmas decorations, it also gives the floral designer special opportunities. Natural materials such as plants, flowers, nuts and fruits can be used in profusion to increase the sense of celebration and welcome, and the florist can feel free of having to arrange flowers alone. Fruit and nuts also have the advantage of staying fresh over a long Christmas season. Other materials with a long life span are cherry laurel, ivy, bun moss and gray lichen moss.

Decorations to last more than one Christmas can be made from dried flowers, preserved leaves and branches, or dried pasta shapes (painted or natural, wheaty cream and spinach green). Wood shavings and raffia tied in bushels or bows make unusual tree decorations that can be brought out year after year.

For many people a door wreath is one of the most important decorations of the season, but these need not look tired and unimaginative, as is too often the case. One can bring a traditional holly or pine garland up to date with a huge tartan, polka-dot or other patterned fabric bow, or incorporate firs and mosses for a country look. Wreaths can even be made of twisted vines or branches, or of dried broom rings entwined with herbs.

A Thanksgiving door decoration looks good made from the same basic wreath with pine foliage replaced by autumn leaves, and including artichokes and gourds instead of pine cones.

Because Christmas is so traditional, it can be easy to get locked into certain set ideas. A way to escape this is to look at other countries and cultures. For example, one day a display of Matrioshkas (Russian nesting dolls) in the window of the Russian Tourist Board in London caught my eye and inspired me to look into the Christmas customs of Eastern Europe. I discovered that wooden figures and brightly painted miniature wooden replicas of everyday cooking and gardening utensils are used to decorate the tree, along with nuts and pine cones, with cinnamon sticks, cloves and nutmeg bound together in little bags of muslin to give a deliciously spicy aroma. I have since incorporated these features into some of my designs.

The centerpiece of Christmas is, of course, the tree, and my favorite type is the blue spruce. It has thick bushy foliage, a wonderful perfume, and should survive the Christmas period better than many other varieties. Branches from this tree lend themselves to lovely settings, say around candles, and I also enjoy experimenting with tree shapes and forms by building my own tree. Starting with a small log cemented vertically into a pot (of the right dimensions for the finished tree), I enclose a ball of damp moss in chicken wire, attach this to the top with wire and drive blue spruce branches into it. From this base any shape can be created of varying size and density. One can make the "perfect" conically shaped tree which I have found is paradoxically guaranteed to make people believe they have discovered a "real" Christmas tree.

Bringing Christmas into a guest room with dried wheat and variegated ivy, together with pine cones, moss and pine set into florists' foam.

BIRTHDAY BREAKFASTS

A leisurely breakfast, especially one prepared by somebody else, is a rare luxury for most of us today, and is usually enjoyed only at home on birthdays or, for a busy mother, on Mother's Day. No one, however, wants too much of a shock first thing in the morning, so modesty in the size of the display is in order.

Doris pinks, Carol roses and blue cornflowers, making pretty pastels for a summer breakfast.

Blue grape hyacinths (muscari) and gypsophila – clean and bright for a spring morning.

RIGHT: *For the really special birthday or Mother's Day treat, a champagne breakfast with equally sparkling narcissi and genista (broom).*

MAKING A MARK WITH SIMPLICITY

An effective way to make an arrangement really stand
out in a crowded room is to go for a simple color
scheme, provided that the flowers are stylish themselves. Because parties almost always involve crowds,
white lilies are nearly always a good choice.

LEFT: *A straight-sided glass bowl filled with water, a candle and three white lilies, for a table at a buffet party.*

RIGHT: *A strong focal point for a party provided by white auratum lilies in a glass vase, placed on a pillar that has been draped with a white cloth. Strands of ivy complete the Arcadian look.*

BELOW: *The same arrangement without the dark green ivy. The greater prominence accorded to the drapery produces an overall softer feel.*

NEW DIMENSIONS

Dramatic flowers can certainly help make a party different, especially if a surrealist touch is introduced. The arrangements shown here, however, would only be appropriate for a sophisticated occasion.

LEFT: *A Greek plate with apples, greengages, grapes, moss, green amaranthus (love-lies-bleeding), red berries and sedum.*

Odd room features can often be exploited with success. Here a wall recess in an art gallery has stimulated an apt idea. Ivy trails from the edge of the frame, while the vase is set well back.

DESIGNING WITH SCENT

These highly scented flowers were selected for the launch of a new perfume at the Ritz Hotel in London. The organizers chose the use of scent in religion as their theme, hence both the particular flowers and the large church candles set in wrought-iron stands.

Lily of the valley, tuberoses, lilac, white anemones, genista (broom), lichen moss and ivy around the church candles on a church candle stand.

White roses, genista (broom), tuberoses and lilac – chosen for their strong scent – in a large perfume bottle.

The same flowers used as a table decoration in another wrought-iron stand.

E A S T E R

Easter used to be a busy time for florists, but is less so now, even though churches are decorated with flowers after Lent. Not necessarily for religious reasons, I find it sad that the custom has declined. There are plenty of fresh spring flowers around and Easter is a holiday when many families spend time at home together.

ABOVE: *Daffodils, hyacinths and catkins marking the arrival of spring.*

RIGHT: *Hen and quail eggs, and bread rolls both introduce traditional elements and suggest the religious celebration. They also create interest along with roses and moss in a basket for a table center.*

DOOR WREATHS

Door wreaths are a traditional way of announcing
Christmas celebrations within, but are also suitable
for other winter festivities such as Hallowe'en and
Thanksgiving.

LEFT: *Both green and variegated holly mixed with lichen, bun moss and a mixture of pines, bring a surprising feeling of festivity to an ancient gate.*

ABOVE: *Winter branches, painted white and twisted into a wreath, then garlanded with strands of ivy, longiflorum lilies and a white satin bow.*

ABOVE: *Blue spruce, with groups of large pine cones and entwined with ivy sprayed gold and silver.*

LEFT: *The most traditional type of all door wreaths, made of berried holly but given originality by the large polka-dot bow.*

FIRST IMPRESSIONS

When entertaining for any special festival it is desirable
to set the mood right away with a special display in the
entrance hall. Shelves, mirrors and side tables can all
be pressed into service, but a blank bit of wall or the
door can also be used for a wreath, which does not have
to look Christmassy.

LEFT: *Twisted branches entwined around the handle of a basket filled with artichokes, eggplants, pine cones, moss and Brussels sprouts set in a large hallway to welcome guests to a winter party.*

RIGHT: *A frosting of ivy sprayed gold tumbles from the top of pillars on either side of a hallway so as to emphasize their classical look.*

BELOW: *The elaborate gilt mirror seemed to be a "must" for a colorful garland and wreath of pines, fir, pine cones, ivy, berries and ornamental peppers for a Christmas party.*

CANDLES

Candles traditionally add a touch of romance and relaxation to any dinner party table setting, especially in winter time. This mood is enhanced by the addition of a natural surround, although foliage and leaves are often enough without flowers.

ABOVE: *A midwinter setting of thick white candles surrounded by auratum lilies, white genista (broom), pine cones and variegated pittosporum.*

LEFT: *Arrangement for a late autumn evening with preserved green magnolia leaves interspersed with the brown of other leaves and small pine cones to tone with the color of a checkered wood table.*

Traditional Christmas colors
of red and green, with pine
branches, variegated holly,
pine cones and driftwood set
around the candles. The
stripped table top invited a
loose and informal
arrangement.

= 141 =

FESTIVE KITCHENS

Busy cooks spend a great deal of time in the kitchen at Christmas and Thanksgiving but that does not mean they have to miss out on the atmosphere of festivity. Modest and chunky accessories are better in a working kitchen than the more intricate ones used elsewhere, especially in conjunction with dominant architectural features like a disused fireplace.

LEFT: *A garland of blue spruce frames the old fireplace that now serves as a home for wine.*

ABOVE: *Features taken from Eastern European customs – miniature wooden spoons and forks together with garlic cloves and red berries – provide variety and a splash of color on the pine branches.*

ABOVE: *Fruit, fir cones and berries, as an alternative embellishment for the pine, suggesting end-of-the-year abundance, are well suited for winter celebrations like Christmas and Thanksgiving.*

LEFT: *Small tree to accompany the garland, made of blue spruce wired into a moss sphere, together with cones and berries, with garlic to match the culinary background.*

CHRISTMAS COLORS

Traditionally, red and green go together at Christmas, probably because of the red berries on the green holly. The wish to stick to these colors need not straitjacket the floral designer; even with the limited variety of flowers available at this time of year, there is still a considerable range of effects possible, whether the display is simple or intricate.

LEFT: *The little "trees" on the mantelpiece are in fact made from fingers of blue spruce wired into a ball of moss, with dried red roses bunched and placed regularly between them. A garland of foliage, some sprayed gold and silver, frames the hearth which is itself filled with a basket of both fresh and dried materials.*

ABOVE: *A deliberately stark effect for a display that is not designed to be a centerpiece. It consists of red gladioli and tall winter branches covered with lichen.*

LEFT: *Berried ivy, a mixture of firs and pine, red amaryllis and poinsettia bracts, placed with a minimum of artifice in a jug.*

AUTUMN
AND WINTER
FESTIVITIES

Although fresh cut flowers are not abundant, nor cheap, in the late autumn and winter, one need not despair of producing displays, whether for an ordinary party or special occasions like Thanksgiving, Christmas or Harvest Festival. Dried flowers come into their own at this time of year, and foliage, fruit and vegetables provide opportunities for unusual arrangements.

ABOVE: *Only dried materials have been used to fill this basket: pine cones, moss, poppy heads and roses.*

LEFT: *Here both fresh and dried materials fill a basket, but without a single fresh flower. Pine cones, seed pods, amaranthus (love-lies-bleeding), gourds, moss, proteas and Chinese lanterns provide the dried elements. Fresh pine has been added for a Christmas feel, but it could easily be removed after the festivities to leave a warm winter arrangement.*

RIGHT: *A wonderfully rich mixture of fresh fruit and vegetables, moss dyed deep purple, and purple arum lilies (Zantedeschia rehmanii) arranged on a wicker tray.*

LETTING IMAGINATION RIP

Sometimes as a florist you are given a brief that enables you to let your imagination run wild – or perhaps you just persuade the customer to let you indulge yourself! To make such occasions work, though, you have to have a sense of theater.

ABOVE: *A single arum lily (Zantedeschia aethiopica) and some ivy in a room setting that could have come from Miss Havisham's room in Dickens' Great Expectations.*

RIGHT: *Blood-red roses and carnations among asparagus fern (plumosus) fill a vase on a gold-colored wrought-iron pedestal decorated with fruit and brocade. The entrance is* *framed with the same fabric. The flowers attempt to match the deliberately "over the top" look of this fashionable night club.*

GIFTS

Tulips, roses, genista (broom) and foliage in a tied bunch, otherwise known as a continental or hostess bouquet. Just undo the bow and it is ready to put in a vase.

Flowers are a time-honored gift, and always seem to be well received, especially when another type of gift might be inappropriate because it is too permanent or too personal. However, as with everything to do with flowers, there is a number of options about how the flowers should be arranged, and a little thought will always make the gift that much more appreciated.

A bouquet is probably the most popular form of floral gift. The flowers are laid flat against a background of foliage, and the bouquet is built up by gradually decreasing the length of the stem to create a shape similar to an old-fashioned wheatsheaf. One

should avoid the tendency to "overwrap:" clear cellophane with a ribbon tying the stems together where they cross at the base is sufficient. Many bouquets are ruined by trails of cheap plastic ribbon.

A bouquet is fine to give to someone who is likely to enjoy arranging their flowers him- or herself in his or her own vases, but an arrangement (usually supported by florists' foam) in a basket or other container is an

RIGHT: *This interesting rustic basket would have made an appealing gift on its own, but is even more so when filled with heads of sedum and climbing roses.*

= *150* =

healthy, but a journey home in the back seat or trunk of a car and another alien air-conditioned or centrally heated environment is often enough to finish them off. Of course, some only shed foliage to grow back stronger than before.

A most important point when ordering flowers is to think about the kind of person you are giving them to, and to ask the florist to interpret your description in their choice of flowers and arrangement. For example, an elderly person would probably appreciate a traditional display of an established, long-lasting variety such as chrysanthemum, but a young student may be more likely to enjoy bright, vibrant colors or fashionable all-white flowers in an exuberant arrangement.

A flower gift can carry a special message in its design. I was once asked to make a "thank-you" present for a young man's parents who had given him a holiday in the Seychelles. He wanted it to reflect the beauty of the island so I created a miniature version using sand, coral and shells, with bougainvillea and exotic native flowers.

The impact of a gift of flowers is not determined by its size: five miniature roses mixed with gypsophila and foliage can be as breathtaking in their daintiness as fifty long-stemmed roses are in their splendor. Men could make a romantic and nostalgic gesture by ordering a thirties- or fifties-style corsage of orchids or gardenias, to be delivered boxed and ribboned. Well, it seemed to do the trick in Hollywood!

ideal present for anyone who would have difficulty in doing this themselves. For example, a hospital patient might not be able to or even allowed to; the host or hostess of a party or wedding would probably be too busy entertaining guests, and a bouquet would only get as far as the kitchen sink. All the flowers will need is watering every other day to help preserve their original appeal.

Another "easy" flower gift is a tied bunch, sometimes known as a "continental bunch" or "hostess bouquet." In this arrangement the full length of the flowers' stems is spiral-bound at one point to form a posy shape of blooms. They can simply be placed in a vase as they are.

A longer-lasting gift can be made of a planted bowl or basket of small flowering and/or non-flowering plants. One should, of course, select plants that enjoy the same light and temperature conditions and soil type if they are to cohabit happily. For example, a green fern or ivy may look good with a cyclamen but they need different room temperatures and have different watering requirements, so the recipient of such a mixture would have to re-pot the plants immediately.

Larger, mature plants such as crotons make good gifts, but be careful to choose a healthy specimen. Many large plants have been shipped from other continents in less than ideal traveling conditions. When they reach the florist they no doubt still look

FAR LEFT: *A small basket makes a good container for any floral gift. This contains roses and cornflowers mixed with statice* (Limonium latifolium) *and variegated pittosporum foliage.*

LEFT BELOW: *A small arrangement is often easier to position than a tall one. Here the flowers are roses, amaryllis, genista (broom), Doris pinks and statice* (Limonium latifolium).

Euphorbia fulgens, *lilies, poppies, ranunculus and brown catkins spilling from a varnished basket. The arrangement has been designed to make a splash, so although it is basically low, height has been provided by leaving some of the stems fairly long. The stretching* Euphorbia fulgens *also add to the sense of abundance. This gift should make an impact wherever positioned, whether on a coffee-table, a shelf or mantelpiece.*

GIFTS FOR SPECIAL OCCASIONS

There are occasions when something special is required – perhaps for an anniversary, Valentine's Day,
or a birthday. Just a bit of extra trouble will make the
gift that bit more remarkable and appreciated.

LEFT: *A present for a child of a pretty basket of mixed polyanthus garnished with popsicles and candy sticks.*

BELOW: *A posy of white anemones – ideal for a bride on her wedding morning.*

LEFT: *Red roses are customary for Valentine's Day, but with a thought for the loved one with a sweet tooth they are joined by chocolate hearts which have been hung from the ribbon trails.*

FLOWER BASKETS

Basket arrangements are quite a common way of sending gifts, and personally I prefer them to bouquets suffocating in cellophane. Unfortunately, many look as if they were made on some florist's assembly line. They can, however, be individual and informal.

A summer gift, or at least one that suggests a summer rose garden – a mixture of roses both in bud and full bloom.

RIGHT ABOVE: *Longiflorum lilies, lilac, anemones, bouvardia and tuberoses, for an elegant and classical décor.*

RIGHT BELOW: *Miniature roses, soleil d'or narcissi, poppies and antirrhinums – a winter gift of spring flowers.*

= *156* =

FLOWERS BY SEASON

The following chart lists the flowers most commonly used for arrangements. They have been grouped according to their natural growing season, although many flowers can now be obtained from florists' at other times of the year.

Scented flowers are marked with an asterisk (*).

SPRING

WHITE	*Amelanchier canadensis*; Arum lily (*Zantedeschia aethiopica*)*; *Cytisus albus* (broom); Heather 6-8 ft (*Erica arborea*); Iris "White Exelsior"; *Helleborus orientalis* (ALSO PINK, RED, MAUVE); *Lilium longiflorum**; Lily of the valley*, *Narcissus* "Polarice"; *Spirea arguta* (bridal wreath); Tulip
PINK	*Amaryllis belladonna*; *Bergenia cordifolia purpurea*; *Eremurus elwesii* (foxtail lily) (ALSO WHITE, YELLOW); Flowering currant (ALSO WHITE, RED, YELLOW, GREEN); English iris (ALSO BLUE, PINK); *Primula denticulata* (ALSO MAUVE); *Prunus serrulata* "Spontana" (Japanese cherry); Tulip "Don Quixote"; Tulip "Peach Blossom"
RED	*Anemone coronaria* "De Caen" (ALSO WHITE, PINK, MAUVE); *Euphorbia griffithii* "Fireglow"; Kaffir lily; Polyanthus (ALSO BLUE, YELLOW, RED, PINK, ORANGE, MAUVE, WHITE); *Ranunculus asiaticus* (ALSO ORANGE, YELLOW); Tulip, lily-flowered "Dyanito"; Tulip, triumph "Tambour Maire"; Wallflower (ALSO WHITE, PINK, ORANGE, YELLOW)*
ORANGE	"Bird of paradise" flower (*Strelizia reginae*); *Euphorbia fulgens* (ALSO PINK, WHITE, RED); Tulip "Aladdin"; Tulip, triumph "Invasion"
YELLOW	*Acacia dealbata* (mimosa); Daffodil "Golden Ducat"; *Euphorbia polychroma*; Forsythia; Iris "Yellow Queen"; Primrose; Parrot tulip "Sunshine"
GREEN	*Euphorbia characias*; *Euphorbia marginata*; Hellebore foetidus; Tulip "Viridiflora"; *Vibernum opulus* "Sterile"
BLUE	Grape hyacinth (muscari) (ALSO WHITE); Hyacinth (ALSO WHITE, PINK, RED, ORANGE, YELLOW, MAUVE); Iris; Wood hyacinth (*Endymion nonscriptus*) (ALSO WHITE, PINK)
MAUVE/ PURPLE	Iris "Purpurea"; Honesty (lunaria) (ALSO WHITE); *Primula auricula* (ALSO YELLOW); *Rhododendron augustinii*; Syringa (lilac) (ALSO WHITE)

❀ SUMMER ❀

WHITE	*Anthericum liliago* (St Bernard's lily); Auratum lily; *Buddleia davidii* (ALSO ORANGE, PINK, RED, MAUVE)*; Cape Marigold, African daisy (dimorpotheca); Freesia "Fantasy"*; Jasmine*; Rose "Iceberg" Floribunda; Yarrow (*Achillea ptarmica* "The Pearl")
PINK	Antirrhinum (ALSO WHITE, RED, YELLOW, ORANGE, MAUVE); Lupin (ALSO WHITE, RED, ORANGE, YELLOW, MAUVE AND MIXTURES); Peony (ALSO WHITE, RED, ORANGE, YELLOW, MAUVE); *Phlox paniculata* (ALSO WHITE, RED, MAUVE)*; Pinks (*Dianthus allwoodii* "Doris")*; *Physostegia virginiana* (obedient plant) (ALSO WHITE, MAUVE); Rose "Constance Spry"; Rose "Roulettii"*; Sweet pea (ALSO WHITE, RED, MAUVE)*
RED	*Anthurium andreanum* (tail-flower); Carnations, border (ALSO WHITE, PINK, ORANGE, YELLOW, MAUVE); *Fuschia magellanica* "Gracilis"; *Malus atrosanguinea*; Penstemon (ALSO WHITE); *Primula sieboldii* (ALSO WHITE, MAUVE); Rose "Lilli Marlene" Floribunda; Sweet William (*Dianthus babatus*) (ALSO WHITE, PINK)
ORANGE	*Buddleia globosa*; *Crocosmia masonorum*; Dahlia, various; Lily "Enchantment"; *Primula aurantiaca*; Red hot poker (kniphofia); Rhododendron "Fabia"; Rose "Flower Arrange"*; Rose "Orange Sensation" Floribunda*
YELLOW	Eremurus (foxtail lily); *Iris pseudacorus*; Rose "Evergold", Rose "Masquerade" Floribunda; Spanish iris; Yarrow (*Achillea taygeta* "moonshine"); Yellow loosestrife (*Lysimachia punctata*)
GREEN	*Alchemilla mollis* (lady's mantle); *Moluccella laevis* (bells of Ireland); *Rosa chinensis* "Viridis"; Tobacco flower (nicotiana) (ALSO WHITE, PINK, RED, MAUVE); *Vibernum opulus* "Sterile" (guelder rose); *Zinnia elegans* "Envy"
BLUE	*Brodiaea laxa*; *Campanula latiloba* (ALSO WHITE); Cornflower (*Centaura cyanus*) (ALSO WHITE, PINK, RED, MAUVE); Delphinium (ALSO WHITE, PINK, MAUVE); Dutch iris (ALSO WHITE, MAUVE); Echinops (globe thistle); Larkspur (ALSO WHITE, PINK, MAUVE); Nigella (love-in-a-mist) (ALSO WHITE, PINK, MAUVE)
MAUVE/ PURPLE	Allium (ALSO WHITE, PINK, RED); Aster (ALSO WHITE, PINK, RED); *Buddleia altenifolia**; *Campanula glomerata*; Dahlia, various; Foxglove (*Digitalis purpurea*) (ALSO WHITE, PINK, RED, ORANGE, YELLOW); Freesia "Cote d'Azur"*; Lavender (*Lavendula spica* "Hidcote")*; Monkshood (Aconitum) (ALSO WHITE, BLUE); Rose "Blue Moon"; Scabious (ALSO WHITE, PINK); Stock (*Matthiola incana*) (ALSO WHITE, PINK, RED)*

AUTUMN

WHITE	*Anemone japonica* (ALSO PINK); *Chrysanthemum bosmariense*; *Chrysanthemum carinatum* "Northern Star"*; *Chrysanthemum maximum* "Esther Read" (Shasta daisy); *Hydrangea paniculata* "Grandiflora"; Stephanotis*
PINK	*Aster amellus* (ALSO WHITE, RED, MAUVE); Bell heather (*Erica cinerea*); *Bouvardia domestica* (ALSO WHITE, RED); Dahlia "Fascination"; *Limonium suworowii* (statice. pink); Nerine (ALSO RED)*
RED	*Amaranthus caudatus* (love-lies-bleeding); Chrysanthemum, various*; *Lilium oriental* "Stargazer"*; Mignonette (*Reseda odorata* "Goliath")*; *Sedum spectabile* "Autumn Joy"
ORANGE	Alstroemeria (ALSO PINK, RED, YELLOW, MAUVE); Chrysanthemum, various*; Montbretia; Pot-marigold; Red hot poker (kniphofia) (ALSO YELLOW)
YELLOW	*Chrysanthemum parthenium* "Goldstar"; Dalia "Hoek's Yellow" (small semi-cactus); Gladiolus (ALSO WHITE, PINK, RED, ORANGE, GREEN, MAUVE); *Limonium sinuatum* (statice) (ALSO WHITE, PINK, RED, MAUVE); Rudbeckia (coneflower) (ALSO ORANGE)*; Yarrow (*Achillea filipendulina* "Coronation Gold") (ALSO WHITE, RED)
GREEN	*Amaranthus caudatus* "Viridis" (love-lies-bleeding); *Cobaea scandens* (ALSO MAUVE); Gladiolus "Green Woodpecker"
BLUE	Agapanthus (African lily); *Caryopteris clandondensis*; *Echinops humilis* "Blue Cloud" (globe thistle); *Hydrangea macrophylla* (ALSO PINK)
MAUVE/ PURPLE	*Anemone japonica* (ALSO WHITE, PINK)*; Aster (Michaelmas daisy) (ALSO WHITE, PINK, RED); *Liatris spicata* "Blazing Star"; *Limonium latifolium* (statice)

WINTER

WHITE	Heather (*Erica hyemalis*)*; *Helleborus niger* (Christmas rose)
PINK	Cyclamen (ALSO WHITE, RED, MAUVE); Laurustinus (*Vibernum tinus*); Protea; *Vibernum fragrans**
RED	*Euphorbia fulgens*
ORANGE	Hyacinth (ALSO WHITE, PINK, YELLOW, BLUE, MAUVE)*
YELLOW	*Cornus mas* (cornelian cherry); *Hamamelis mollis* (Chinese witch hazel)*; Winter-flowering jasmine (*Jasminum nudiflorum*)
GREEN	*Helleborus foetidus*
BLUE	*Iris reticulata* (ALSO MAUVE)
MAUVE/ PURPLE	*Helleborus orientalis* (lenten rose); *Iris stylosa* (Algerian iris) (ALSO PINK)*

FLOWERS ALL AROUND THE YEAR

The following flowers are available throughout the year. Most species come in a variety of colors.

Alstroemeria (WHITE, PINK, RED, ORANGE, YELLOW, MAUVE)

Anthurium (tail-flower) (WHITE, PINK, RED) • Arum lily (zantedeshcia) (WHITE, PINK, YELLOW)

Chrysanthemum, sprays, single blooms, rayonante (WHITE, PINK, RED, ORANGE, YELLOW, MAUVE)

Cymbidium orchid (WHITE, PINK, RED, ORANGE, YELLOW, GREEN, MAUVE)

Dianthus (spray carnation, carnation) (WHITE, PINK, RED, ORANGE, YELLOW, MAUVE)

Freesia (WHITE, PINK, RED, ORANGE, YELLOW, MAUVE) • Gerbera (WHITE, PINK, RED, ORANGE, YELLOW)

Gladiolus (WHITE, PINK, RED, ORANGE, YELLOW, GREEN, MAUVE) • Gypsophila (WHITE)

Iris (WHITE, PINK, YELLOW, BLUE, MAUVE)

Lily (WHITE, PINK, RED, ORANGE, YELLOW) • Rose (WHITE, PINK, RED, ORANGE, YELLOW, MAUVE)

WHITE "Athena" • PINK "Carol" • RED "Baccara"

ORANGE "Belinda" or "Mercedes" • PEACH "Gerdo" • YELLOW "Evergold"

Singapore orchid (dendrobium) (WHITE, PINK, RED, ORANGE, YELLOW, GREEN, MAUVE)

FOLIAGE

Foliage is largely a matter of picking what you feel
looks right, but the following have proved themselves
to be good mixers.

EVERGREEN

GREEN	Aspidistra; Bamboo; *Bergenia cordifolia*; Box (buxus); Cherry laurel; *Choisya ternata* (Mexican orange); Cotoneaster; Escallonia; *Fatshedera lizei*; *Fatsia japonica*; *Griselinia littoralis*; *Helleborus foetidus*; Laurustinus (*Viburnum tinus*); *Mahonia aquifolium*; *Mahonia japonica*; *Monstera deliciosa*; Papyrus (umbrella plant); *Pittosporum tenuifolium*; Privet; Ruscus; Skimmia; Soft ruscus or Alexandrian laurel (*Danaë racemosa*); Yew
VARIEGATED GREEN/WHITE	Aspidistra "Variegata"; *Euonymus radicans* "Silver Queen"; *Hebe andersonii* "Variegata"; Holly (*Ilex aquifolium* "Silver Queen"); Ivy (*Hedera canariensis* "Variegata"); *Pittosporum tenuifolium* "Irene Paterson"; *Pittosporum tenuifolium* "Silver Queen"
GRAY/GREEN AND SILVER	*Cupressus glabra* "Pyramidalis"; *Eucalyptus gunni*; *Garrya elliptica*; *Hebe pagei*; *Helichrysum angustifolium* (curry plant); Rosemary; Rue (*Ruta graveolens* "Jackmans Blue"); *Santolina chamaecyparissus* (cotton lavender); Senecio cineraria maritima; *Senecio laxifolius* "Sunshine"; Western hemlock (*Tsuga heterophylla*)
RED, BRONZE AND PURPLE	*Begonia rex*; *Bergenia cordifolia*; *Hebe speciosa* "Mrs Winder"; *Mahonia aquifolium*; *Ricinus communis* (castor oil plant); *Tellima grandiflora* "Purpurea"
LIME GREEN AND YELLOW	*Aucuba japonica* "Crotonifolium" (spotted laurel); Box (buxus) "Latifolia Maculata"; *Cupressus macrocarpa* "Donard Gold"; *Eleagnus pungens* "Maculata"; *Euonymus japonicus* "Aureus"; *Hebe salicifolia*; Holly (*Ilex* "Golden King"); Honeysuckle (*Lonicera nitida* "Baggesen's Gold"); *Iris pseudacorus* "Variegata"; Ivy (*Hedera colchica* "Dentata"); Ivy (*Hedera helix* "Buttercup"); *Sansevieria trifasciata* "Laurentii" (mother-in-law's tongue); Yew (*Taxus baccata* "Dovastonii Aurea")

DECIDUOUS

GREEN	*Arum italicum* "Pictum"; Contorta hazel; Ferns, various; *Hypericum elatum* "Elstead"; *Phormium tenax* (New Zealand flax); *Yucca*
VARIEGATED GREEN/WHITE	*Acer negundo* "Argenteo Marginatum"; *Acer platanoides* "Drummondii" (Norway maple); *Hosta albo-marginata*; *Iris foetidissima variegata*; Ornamental kale (cabbage); Periwinkle (*Vinca major variegata*)
GRAY/GREEN AND SILVER	*Artemisia ludoviciana* (white sage); Globe artichoke; *Hosta sieboldiana* "Elegans"; *Macleaya microcarpa* (plume poppy); *Onoporon arabicum*; *Stachys lanata* (lamb's tongue)
RED, BRONZE AND PURPLE	*Acer platanoides* "Crimson King" (Norway maple); *Berberis thunbergii* "Atropurpurea"; *Canna hybrida* "America"; Copper beech; *Cotinus coggygria* "Velvet Cloak" (smoke tree); Fennel (*Foeniculum vulgare*); *Ligularia dentata* "Desdemona" (golden ray); *Physocarpus opulifolius* "Luteus"; *Prunus cerasifera* "Atropurpurea" (cherry plum); *Rosa rubrifolia*; *Vitis coignetiae* (Japanese crimson glory vine)
LIME GREEN AND YELLOW	*Acer japonicum* "Aureum"; Golden privet; Hosta "golden medallion"; *Physocarpus opulifolius* "Luteus"; *Sambucus racemosa* "Plumosa aurea" (golden elder)

The following types of foliage are usually commercially
available from good florists:

Aspidistra • Blue spruce • Croton • Eucalyptus • Holly • Ivy • Ruscus
• Soft ruscus or Alexandrian laurel (*Danaë racemosa*) • Various
ferns • Western hemlock

In addition many types of preserved material are sold,
for instance beech, palm leaves and various ferns and
grasses.

CARING FOR FLOWERS

Two carnations, one (right) still young and vigorous, the other aging with its stigmas exposed.

In this section I intend to destroy a few myths concerning flower care and buying, and pass on some observations and advice which I hope will benefit anyone regularly buying fresh flowers.

Flowers bought from a market stall or vendor are usually much cheaper than those from a florist, but a good florist can give better service and offer both a wider selection of flowers and ones of higher quality. It is possible to find real bargains in a flower stall, but in my experience the traders choose their stock by the best prices at market rather than by the best produce. Also, vendors have to store their flowers overnight in vans or elsewhere in all weather conditions, and naturally the flowers suffer.

Even worse for storage, though, are department stores that cash in on the growing popularity of fresh flowers and plants, and give floristry a bad name by neglecting the storage conditions of their stock. Many of them rely only on a fast turnover to be able to offer freshness; any flowers they have not sold almost immediately are likely to be suffering from the poor way in which they have been kept.

When flicking through a recently published flower book I saw to my horror that it cautioned against buying flowers on a Monday as it claimed that they would undoubtedly be leftovers from the previous week. How misguided this is! In fact Monday is one of the best trading days in the world's flower markets, with flowers coming in from all over the world for the new week. It is certainly the busiest day in my shop.

It is a florist's lot to be

accused sometimes of using "old" flowers in bouquets and arrangements. I would never indulge in such a practice, and most other respectable florists would not either. However, there are times when absolutely fresh flowers would be unsuitable for the job. For instance, a table arrangement for a lunch or dinner that will last five or six hours at the most demands considerable skill from the florist in selecting blooms at varying and appropriate stages of development. Using tightly budded flowers would be pointless as the guests will not be around long enough to witness the beauty of the flowers in full bloom, two days later. But selecting only fully opened blooms is not the answer either, as some of them might wilt before the meal is over. A combination of mature and youthful flowers is usually the right mix. Some of the arrangements in this book would not be suitable for the home arranger, precisely for this reason, that they were done for a specific occasion and were not planned to last until the next day.

For a bouquet the same rules generally apply. If it is a gift, one should always include a balanced selection of flowers of different ages so that they look attractive both on delivery and when the tightly budded flowers open in the home. If you want flowers for your home that will last into the following week you should tell the florist and be prepared not to purchase wide-open blooms. Spring flowers especially cannot be expected to have a very long life, so they shouldn't be bought open or nearly open.

There are many clues to the freshness of flowers. Carnations, although long-lasting, have easily recognizable signs of age. The center of the bloom becomes soft to the touch, exposing two white stigmas, and the tips of the petals begin to curl inwards as if the bud had just opened. It is the foliage of chrysanthemums that gives the best indication of when they were cut. If the leaves are drooping and turning yellow, or if the foliage has been completely stripped by the florist, they are unlikely to be fresh. Lilies have slightly transparent petals when past their best.

The time lapse between a flower's being cut at the nursery and its arrival at the retailer can vary considerably. Therefore it is essential for florists to condition the flowers properly and for the buyer to do the same at home in order to extend their lifespan. The stems of most flowers simply require cutting about an inch and a half up from their base, at an angle to present the greatest surface area to the water. Treatment can vary according to

The bloom looks fine, but the foliage shows this chrysanthemum is fading.

Fresh leaves indicate this chrysanthemum should last for some time.

Aging lily, whose petals have become translucent.

A young lily in good condition with firm, opaque petals

variety. In general, woody and fibrous stems such as chrysanthemums or honeysuckle should be cut and hammered with a wooden mallet at the base so they absorb more water. Blooms from poppies or euphorbias will have been treated when cut by searing the base of the stem with a flame to prevent the release of a milky fluid that restricts water intake, and the stems should not be recut unless the same process is repeated. Spring bulbs and corms — for example, narcissi, daffodils and hyacinths — will bleed a sap-like fluid when cut and further cutting should be avoided. If, however, it is unavoidable so as to fit them into a particular vase, cutting them under water will prevent excess leakage.

The thick tubular stems of amaryllis and lupins collapse if not conditioned correctly. They should be held upside-down, their hollow stems filled with water and plugged with absorbent cotton or tissue. Before arranging they should be placed in a bucket of hand-warm water.

Long-stemmed roses need to be conditioned each time they are taken out of water for any length of time to prevent the heads from drooping before the buds have fully opened. Drooping is not a sign of old age, but an indication that water isn't being drawn up to the head. The flowers should be placed in deep water after trimming the stems, and never arranged in a short vase. If they begin to show signs of flagging, the stems should be recut and the flowers laid flat on a piece of paper with their heads in line with the stems. After they have been wrapped tightly and returned to water for a couple of hours, the stems will become strong and erect again.

Tulips will always bend towards the source of light. I like to see this effect, with the flowers sweeping

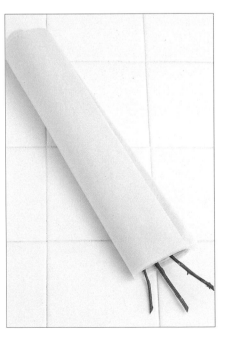

down from the container and then up to a light source. If you don't like this, turn the container at intervals to keep the stems upright, and condition them in the same way as described for roses.

Delicately stemmed violets often appear weak and tired when bought; completely submerging them in a bowl of water for a couple of hours at most will revitalize them.

Whenever one has to buy flowers a day or so before their intended use, it is advisable to keep them in a cool environment, but not in a household refrigerator. It is far too cold, and although they seem to be keeping fresh and intact, once the flowers are returned to room temperature the petals will quickly look singed and transparent.

Spraying with a water mister will freshen most flowers up, but shouldn't be used on orchids as the petals will become transparent and badly stained.

Vase water needs to be changed at least every one or two days, especially for softer-stemmed flowers. Remove any foliage from the stem area that will be immersed in water as it will decompose and cause the water to discolor, which results in shorter flower life. There are many proprietary brands of water additives that claim to keep flowers fresh and longer-lasting. I rarely use them and am doubtful about their real value, but many respected florists do use them and all I can advise is to try them yourself.

TOP: *A stem should be cut at the angle that gives the largest surface area.*

MIDDLE: *A fibrous stem lightly hammered to make it more absorbent.*

BOTTOM: *Roses wrapped in newspaper so as to straighten them. They should be wrapped firmly, but not so tightly as to damage the heads.*

INDEX